Sell Your Horse The Right Way

A practical guide to pricing fairly, placing horses well, and making decisions you can stand behind

Jeanette Gower

Note: anywhere "he" is used, this includes "she" and "they."

ISBN – Hard Cover: 9798258542915

ISBN - Paperback: **978-1-968253-82-0**

ISBN - Ebook : B0GWWP6MTD

First edition published in Australia.

Contents

Foreword

The decisions that stay with you

Have you ever advertised a horse, only to find it takes forever to generate an enquiry, or if it does, there is no further action? Have you ever watched as another very similar horse, of similar quality and training, sells quickly and for the same price, or even better, than yours?

There is a particular frustration that arises when good horses do not sell well. It is not often spoken about, perhaps because it feels uncomfortable to question the process when the horses themselves have been raised with care. They are well bred, well handled, and given time and attention.

Still, they do not always sell easily.

They attract interest that goes nowhere, remain on the market longer than expected, or are quietly passed over while other similar horses sell quickly and without apparent effort. Over time, that contrast can erode confidence and leave sellers wondering what they are missing.

Selling a horse is rarely just a transaction.

A horse is advertised. A buyer appears. Money changes hands. The horse moves on. Yet anyone who has been through the process more than once knows that beneath that simplicity sits a tangle of responsibility, expectation, emotion, and consequence.

Horses are not simply objects. They carry history, training, limitations, habits, and often a great deal of human investment. When a horse is sold, all of that moves with them, whether it is acknowledged or not.

The quality of that transition matters.

Many people approach selling with uncertainty because the rules are unclear. Advice is contradictory. One person tells you to say less. Another tells you to disclose everything. Somewhere in the middle, you are expected to make decisions that affect not just you, but the animal and the person on the other side of the sale.

Not by offering shortcuts or guarantees, but by slowing the process down and examining where decisions are made, how pressure shows up, and what actually holds a sale together over time.

This book is written for people who want to sell horses responsibly, protect everyone involved, and make choices they can live with long after the horse truck has left the driveway.

What you will find is a way of thinking clearly, communicating honestly, and recognising where restraint matters more than enthusiasm.

Selling horses well depends on alignment between the horse, the buyer, the seller, and the method of sale.

When that fit is present, sales tend to hold together quietly.

When it is missing, problems tend to unravel later, often in ways that could have been prevented.

Sell Your Horse The Right Way follows the process from the beginning to the end, from you deciding whether to sell at all, through advertising, contact, evaluation, vetting, contracts, special sales, to finally what happens after the sale is complete. Along the way, it addresses the practical realities that are often glossed over, including pressure from buyers, competing interests, illness or injury mid process, and the moments where selling is not the right answer.

Selling horses well rests on ethics, knowledge, and judgement.

Introduction

As a horse breeder and rider, I have bred, bought, sold, and placed horses for many decades.

Like most people who stay in this industry long enough, I have made good decisions and poor ones, sometimes with the same horse. I have learned that when things go wrong, it is rarely because the horse itself failed. More often, the failure sits in the process that brought horse and human together.

Over time, that realisation changes how you approach selling.

Selling a horse is rarely about the horse alone, and many capable breeders and owners struggle not because they are doing things badly, but because they are walking the wrong path to their buyer. Most sellers genuinely want the best outcome for their horses. They are not careless or indifferent. They act with good intent.

Tried and true methods do exist but they are not widely understood.

The problem is that most people never sell enough horses to learn the art of selling through repetition. A breeder may only sell a handful of horses each year. An owner may sell one or two in a lifetime. And when circumstances change, through health, finances, or life events, the process is often rushed, and decisions are made under pressure.

Horses, meanwhile, do not always cope well with change. Many do not transition easily into radically different environments, routines, or expectations. A move from a quiet property to a busy riding school, from a familiar handler to an inexperienced one, or from consistent work to inconsistency can unravel even a well intentioned placement.

How do you weigh what you know about the horse against what a buyer hopes for?

How do you decide when to proceed, when to pause, and when not to sell at all?

What tools are at your disposal to sell your horse without regret?

These questions sit at the heart of this book.

Too many horses pass through low end saleyards or disappear into systems that do not serve them well. Too many are bred without a realistic future in mind.

The responsibility of the seller is not to guarantee a perfect outcome. That is not possible. The responsibility is to maximise the chances of the horse being placed in a situation where it can thrive, and to make decisions that stand up over time.

Why I wrote this book

Too many owners feel uncertain when it comes time to sell their horse. Much of the advice available is anecdotal, emotionally charged, or shaped by markets that reward speed rather than judgement. Over time, I have watched capable, thoughtful horse owners lose confidence in their own decision making.

I have seen good horses placed poorly, through rushed processes and unspoken assumptions. I have also seen sellers carry regret long after a sale, myself included, wondering whether they should have asked different questions, paused longer, or trusted their instincts more.

This book was written to give you a clearer approach to decision making, to give you tools and checklists for a successful sale.

Sell Your Horse The Right Way offers a way of thinking, to recognise where clarity matters as much as kindness, where firmness protects rather than alienates, and where responsibility does not end simply because ownership changes. This book exists to support that responsibility.

It is written as a companion to *Buy The Right Horse*. That book asks buyers to slow down, assess honestly, and take responsibility for the choices they make.

Between them sits the place where most problems arise, not through malice, but through mismatch.

If this book helps you to think more clearly, and place horses more thoughtfully, then I am pleased to say it has done its work.

– Jeanette

Chapter 1

Selling a horse is not simply a transaction

Why responsibility does not end when the truck leaves

Most people begin selling a horse by telling themselves a simple story. The horse no longer fits quite as well as it once did. Life has changed. Someone else will have more time, more resources, or a clearer purpose. These explanations are incomplete.

Selling a horse is often treated as a straightforward exchange, a practical reshuffling of circumstances. Money changes hands, ownership transfers, and the horse moves on. Yet if you have sold more than one horse, you know that the effects of a sale rarely end at the gate. What follows can be smooth and unremarkable, or it can unravel slowly, months later, in ways that are hard to reverse .

A horse does not leave its history behind when it leaves your property.

It takes its training, its habits, its sensitivities, and its expectations with it. It carries the effects of how it was handled, what it learned to tolerate, and how pressure was applied or relieved. When you sell a horse, you are not just selling an animal in the present moment. You are transferring lived experience into someone else's care.

This is why sales that look perfectly acceptable on paper can falter long after the float has pulled away, while others that seem ordinary at the time quietly succeed. The difference is not usually luck. It is alignment.

A good sale is one where the horse, the buyer, and the circumstances fit together not only at the point of sale, but long after the horse has left. That kind of fit does not occur by accident. It is shaped by the decisions a seller makes long before a buyer commits, and by the way responsibility is understood and carried throughout the process.

One of the reasons selling horses feels so fraught is that you are often encouraged to focus on outcomes instead of responsibility. Price achieved. Speed of sale. Number of enquiries. These measures do not indicate whether a placement will last. They do not account for what the horse will be asked to do next, or whether the buyer's reality truly matches the horse's needs.

The horse world is full of stories about sales that went wrong, yet most do not begin with dishonesty or bad intent. They begin with assumptions that were never examined. With things left unsaid because they felt awkward or inconvenient, or optimism for the sale is allowed to override judgement.

When you treat the transaction as the finish line, you are more likely to rush, soften boundaries, or assume details will resolve later. In practice, those details rarely do.

When you see the sale as a transfer of responsibility, it changes how you handle everything else.

It changes how you prepare the horse, because you are not just presenting it well, you are deciding whether it is genuinely ready for change. It changes how you communicate with buyers, because you are not trying to persuade them, you are trying to understand them. And it changes how you understand success, because a quiet, uneventful transition becomes more meaningful than a fast or impressive one.

You do not carry lifelong responsibility for horses you no longer own. However, it does mean recognising clearly that the choices you make during the selling process have consequences that extend beyond the moment of exchange.

A horse cannot advocate for itself in a sale. That responsibility sits with the seller, whether it is acknowledged or not.

When you understand this, selling does not become harder. It becomes clearer. It replaces vague unease with deliberate decisions. It allows you to approach the process not as something to get through, but as something to do well.

And that shift, underpins everything that follows.

Chapter 2

Why are you selling?

The consequences of getting this wrong

Most people assume the practical decisions are the hard part of selling a horse. The price. The advert. The photographs. The vet check. These are tangible, visible steps, and they give the impression that progress is being made.

What is far more influential is why you are selling the horse in the first place.

That reason matters, but does not need to be shared publicly. It does need to be understood honestly by you. If you gloss over this step, or tell yourself a version of the story that feels more acceptable than accurate, the sale process usually becomes more complicated than it needs to be.

People sell horses for many reasons. A change in direction, a rider who has outgrown the horse, an injury (either theirs or the horse's), a shift in finances or time, an athletic horse that is too quick for its owner and confidence has been lost, breeding stock being moved on as part of a program.

Some sales are planned and unemotional. Others arrive suddenly and carry a great deal of weight.

If you are selling under pressure, you will behave differently, often without realising it. Urgency narrows your judgement. It makes certain compromises feel reasonable that would otherwise raise concern. You may soften boundaries, overlook misalignment, or accept reassurances you would normally question, because you want the situation resolved

At the other end of the spectrum, if you are not particularly motivated to sell, you can sabotage the process Prices drift upward. You answer enquiries half-heartedly. Suitability criteria shift depending on the day. Buyers sense this ambivalence quickly, even if they cannot articulate it, and many step away quietly rather than challenge it.

Ask yourself what will make this sale feel successful six months from now, not just financially, but emotionally. Would a slower sale to the right home feel better than a fast sale that leaves you uneasy? Would holding firm on price matter more than seeing the horse settled and progressing? These questions shape how you respond to buyers, how you present the horse, and how much pressure you place on yourself to accept a particular outcome.

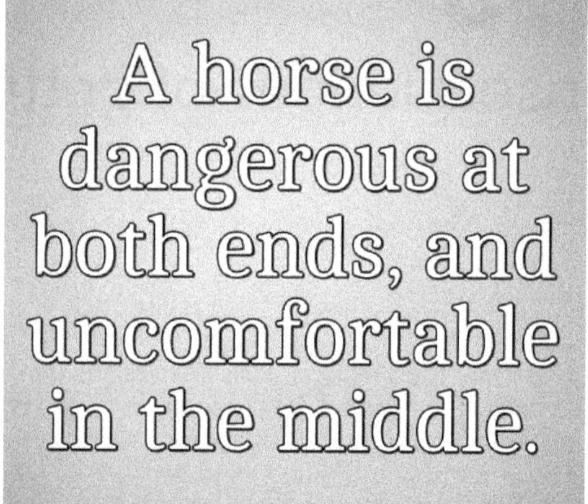

Why are you selling?

There is also an important distinction between selling because you want to and selling because you must. When necessity drives the sale, it becomes more important to create structure around the process. Clear pricing. Clear suitability criteria. Clear boundaries around what you will and will not accept. Structure becomes a buffer between urgency and regret.

You may believe that being transparent about your reasons for selling will undermine your position. In practice, over-explaining creates risk. Buyers do not need the full backstory. They need to understand the horse in front of them and whether it fits their life. Your motivation matters primarily because it influences your judgement, not because you must disclose it.

This is also where emotion quietly enters the picture. Selling a horse you care about often involves grief, even when the decision is rational and necessary. That grief does not override the decision, but it does deserve acknowledgment. Ignoring it tends to make it surface later as doubt, hesitation, or second guessing at precisely the wrong moment.

Clarity about why you are selling makes you steadier. It allows you to recognise when pressure is influencing your decisions and when hesitation signals something that needs attention. It helps you distinguish between discomfort that comes from letting go and discomfort that comes from misalignment.

Why is she selling?

How assumptions distort reality.

A friend of the seller was asked why they were selling such a beautiful horse. The friend says "she doesn't like her."

"How do you know that?" was the reply. "She told me. She doesn't like riding her because she answers to lateral aids instead of diagonal ones. Either she has to change the way she rides, or change the way the horse does everything."

That's quite different, *and important.* It is how Chinese whispers develop.

Seller forgot to mention

We had a seller come to us because she was going through divorce. We knew the horse because we broke her in about four years back. She just wanted a quick sale, without going through advertising and vetting buyers, even though she knew we'd move her on.

She gave us a good deal because we ended up paying the price she paid when she bought her from us.

However, when my daughter rode the mare she had no mouth, and had lost all concept of bending. It turns out she had been ridden all that time in a halter. The seller never thought to mention it.

So the mare had to go through a re-education process before resale. Projects can take much longer than you expect because you find out things you never thought to ask.

Rushed or forced sales due to life changes

Life does not always allow for ideal timing. Illness, financial pressure, family changes, or loss can force a sale before a seller feels ready. In these moments, decision making is often compressed, and the risk of compromise increases.

What matters is recognizing when pressure is influencing your judgement.

Sellers may need to be more realistic about price, firmer about suitability, and clearer about what they can and cannot offer. Attempting to maintain ideal outcomes under urgent conditions can create more stress, not less.

Urgency changes strategy, not responsibility. Acting early and clearly protects the horse far more than waiting until options disappear.

When sellers are clear about their own position, the rest of the process becomes simpler. Communication becomes more consistent. Boundaries feel less arbitrary.

And that clarity, quietly established at the beginning, carries through the entire sale.

Chapter 3

Would you buy your own horse?

The question that reveals everything you need to know

This question can be uncomfortable to answer honestly. It is a question that cuts through optimism, habit, and emotional attachment more efficiently than most others. If you were the buyer, would you buy this horse as it stands today?

Not as you remember it, not as you hope it will be, but as it stands now, at this price, for the purpose you are advertising.

You may think you already know the answer to this, until you consider it properly. As the seller, you live with the horse in a way the buyer never will. We know their good days and their off days. We know what unsettles them, what they tolerate, and what they merely endure. Over time, familiarity can normalize behaviour. Behaviours that would raise questions for an outsider fade from notice.

The buyer does not have that context.

They arrive with limited information, a great deal of hope, and limited tolerance for risk. What feels manageable to you may feel significant to them. What you have learned to work around may look like a deal breaker when viewed without history.

This is where the question becomes practical rather than theoretical

Living with a horse over time changes how you assess it. Behaviours that would stand out to an outsider become familiar. Reactions that once required adjustment become second nature. You learn how to manage the horse, how to set it up for success, and how to avoid situations that bring out its weaker moments.

Gradually you stop noticing what you have learned to work around.

Would you buy this horse knowing what you know about its temperament, its soundness, its management needs, and its response to pressure? Would you buy it for the level and discipline you are recommending? Would you buy it for the type of rider you are trying to attract?

An honest answer may be "no." That "no" matters. It points to something that needs adjustment.

Often what needs to change is not the horse, but the way it is being positioned.

A horse that is priced as though it is straightforward, but behaves like one that requires confidence and consistency, creates doubt. A horse advertised as suitable for progression, but happiest at a steady, repetitive level, creates disappointment. A horse with specific management needs presented as low maintenance creates resentment later.

The problem is rarely the horse itself. It is the gap between expectation and reality.

This is also where price becomes entangled with personal investment. Sellers sometimes ask whether they would buy their own horse at a given price and answer 'yes' instinctively, because they know the work that has gone into producing it. Buyers, however, are not paying for effort. They are paying for outcome and risk.

Potential is only valuable if the buyer is positioned to realise it.

A useful way to approach this question is to imagine yourself as a cautious buyer, not an optimistic one. Imagine you are spending your own money, managing your own risk, and carrying the consequences if things do not work out as planned.

Would the price feel fair? Would the description feel accurate? Would the limitations feel clearly stated or quietly minimised?

If the answer is 'no', something needs to shift.

That shift may be subtle. It may be as simple as changing your target buyer, reframing the horse's strengths, or being more explicit about where it will struggle. In some cases, it may mean waiting, adjusting training, or accepting that the horse fits a narrower market than you hoped.

You know the horse in a way no buyer ever can, while the buyer must make a decision based on fragments, impressions, and trust.

This imbalance is not a problem in itself. It becomes one only if you forget the responsibility that comes with it.

You may worry that being honest with yourself at this level will make selling harder. In practice, it tends to do the opposite. Clear thinking sharpens your communication. It filters enquiries more effectively. It reduces the number of conversations that end in quiet disengagement.

Buyers sense when you have done this work.

They feel it in the way the horse is described, in the consistency of the answers, and in the absence of defensiveness. They may not name it, but they respond to it.

They arrive seeing the horse *as it presents on that day, in that setting, under those conditions*. They do not know which behaviours are consistent and which are situational. They do not know what improves with routine and what requires constant management. They are trying to read a story from a single page.

This is why knowing your horse well is not just an advantage in a sale. It is an *obligation.*

Knowing your horse means understanding more than its strengths. It means being able to describe how it copes when things are imperfect. How it responds to unfamiliar environments. What unsettles it. What it tolerates, and what it genuinely accepts. These distinctions matter more to a buyer than an impressive list of achievements.

Don't confuse familiarity with knowledge. Don't assume that because you have owned the horse for a long time, you understand it fully. Time alone does not create insight. Attention does. Reflection does. Being willing to notice patterns rather than dismiss them does.

When you truly know your horse, you can answer questions without feeling the need for justification, because you are not trying to protect an image.

This is particularly important when it comes to temperament. Temperament is not a fixed trait. It is a relationship between the horse, the rider, and the environment. A horse that feels straightforward in one setting may become tense or resistant in another. A horse that is generous with a familiar rider may feel guarded with someone new.

The same applies to soundness and management. Many horses are perfectly serviceable with appropriate care, but become problematic when that care is inconsistent or misunderstood. A seller who glosses over management needs because they have learned to accommodate them does the horse and buyer no favours.

It is not disloyal to a horse to describe its limitations. In fact, it is one of the most protective things you can do.

When sellers avoid naming difficulties, they often do so out of kindness or fear rather than deception. They do not want to scare buyers away. They do not want the horse to be judged unfairly. They may hope that the right buyer will naturally adjust. Hope is not a strategy.

Knowing your horse well also means understanding where your knowledge ends. There are aspects of a horse's future performance that no seller can predict.

Pretending otherwise creates unrealistic expectations.

It is enough to say what you know, how you know it, and where uncertainty remains. Buyers are not seeking guarantees.

Something that the seller assumed was obvious, unimportant, or not worth mentioning erodes trust, not through what was said, but through what was omitted.

Asking whether you would buy your own horse has another benefit. It creates emotional distance at precisely the point where attachment can cloud judgement. It invites you to step out of the role of owner and briefly into the role of assessor.

Buyers recognise when you are grounded in reality rather than optimism. When you do this well, the right buyer recognises themselves in the description, and the sale progresses more smoothly.

When you embrace this responsibility, you place horses more accurately, buyers make better decisions. And that steadiness carries forward.

That is the quiet power of this question.

Knowing your horse better than your buyer ever will is stewardship.

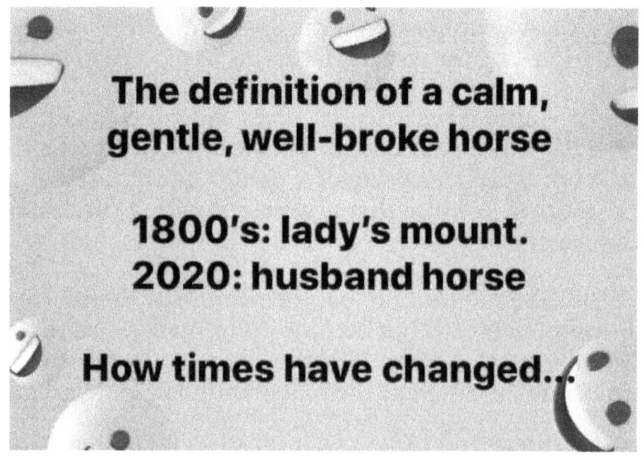

Chapter 4

Preparing the horse

Health, handling, and readiness for sale

Preparation is one of those words that sounds simple, yet it carries very different meanings depending on who uses it. For some sellers, preparing a horse means polishing what is already there. For others, it means rushing to present something that is not quite ready and hoping the cracks do not show.

Preparation begins well before you advertise it. Six to eight weeks is a realistic minimum, not because it guarantees a better outcome, but because it allows you to condition the horse fairly rather than hurry it.

A horse prepared for sale has experienced enough variety to cope with change without becoming overwhelmed. You should handle it in a way that reflects how it will be handled next, not just how you handle it now. You place it in a position where its strengths can be seen clearly and its limitations do not come as a surprise.

Health as the foundation

Preparation is not cosmetic. It starts with health. Good preparation works from the inside out.

A horse cannot be assessed honestly if it is not in condition. Before advertising, make sure routine health care is up to date. This includes dentistry, worming based on appropriate testing, and farriery. If you are uncertain about condition or coat quality, allow adequate time for nutritional adjustments. It makes a noticeable difference.

Horses that are comfortable, well fed, and appropriately managed travel better, cope better with inspections, and show their true temperament more reliably.

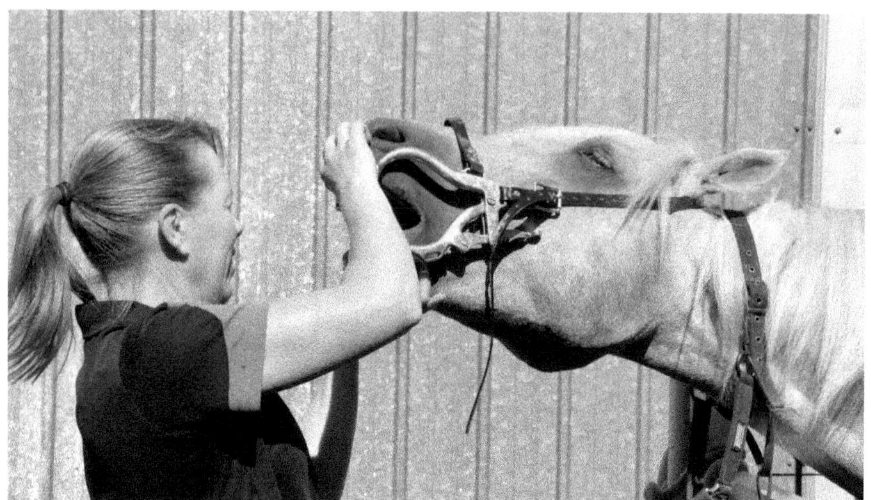

Dental examination as part of sale preparation. Photo: Dr M Newell

Physical readiness

Physical readiness is the most obvious layer, and therefore the easiest to misunderstand. Physical readiness does not mean you overproduce or push the horse to demonstrate its potential. It means the horse is fit enough to do comfortably what you are asking it to demonstrate now.

If you advertise a horse as riding sound, it should be in regular work. If this is not the case, you need time to bring the horse back into work, either with its regular rider or with appropriate professional support.

A horse presented as ready to step into a discipline should be conditioned enough that it can be assessed without guessing what it might turn into months later. Preparation should reflect the demands of the advertised role, not the idealised future version you hope the horse will become.

Mental readiness

Mental readiness is just as important. A horse that copes only within a very narrow routine may struggle when faced with the inevitable disruptions of a sale. New people. New environments. New expectations.

Mental preparation does not mean you expose the horse to everything. It means you expose it enough that it can settle when faced with challenges, rather than escalate under pressure. A horse that recovers when unsettled gives you far more reliable information than one that has never worked outside its comfort zone, such as being ridden off the property, or transported to a veterinary clinic.

Practical readiness

Ownership records, registration details, identification, and veterinary history form part of the horse's story. Make sure they are clear, accurate, and available for discussion. Uncertainty here does not resolve itself later. It compounds.

Practical readiness also means you know what information you will and will not put in writing, and understanding the implications of that decision before the horse is offered for sale.

A well-prepared horse does not need explanation.

When preparation means waiting

You should never use preparation to manufacture a false impression.

If you school the horse harder than usual, ride it beyond its comfort zone, or disguise uncertainty through repetition, you may create a more polished appearance in the moment, but it introduces a mismatch that surfaces quickly after the sale.

If your horse is recovering from injury, unsettled due to recent changes, or lacking condition, wait. That is professionalism.

Preparation clarifies whether the horse is ready to be evaluated now, or whether you need to give it more time.

Preparation checklist

Physical readiness

- The horse is clean, groomed, and presented appropriately for its breed or discipline
- The horse is in regular work and can be demonstrated in line with the role advertised
- Fitness reflects current ability, not future potential
- The horse will stand and trot out for inspection
- Handling under saddle or on the ground is consistent
- The horse can be assessed honestly on the day with the rider or handler and equipment it is normally worked in

Mental readiness

- The horse copes with changes in routine without undue stress

- The horse can be handled or ridden by someone other than you
- The horse loads, ties, and stands reasonably, and allows its feet to be picked up
- The horse recovers when unsettled rather than escalating

Practical readiness

- Ownership is clear and undisputed
- Registration and identification details are accurate
- Veterinary history is known and can be discussed honestly
- Training and competition history is available
- You know what information you will and will not put in writing, including any contractual terms

If the horse is ready, are you?

Is your paperwork available and complete to be shown to a buyer?

Chapter 5

Shaping expectations for a sale

When is the sale ready to proceed?

Once a horse is genuinely ready to be sold, a different responsibility begins.

At this stage, the question is no longer whether the horse is ready. The question is whether you are handling the sale with the same level of care.

Buyers do not assess horses in theory. They assess what is in front of them. Your job is to make sure those two things *align*.

Expectation forms early, often before first contact. Once formed, it is difficult to correct.

Representing the horse accurately

The purpose of advertising is not to persuade. It is to describe. Advertising is not separate from preparation. It exists to support it. If what you describe does not match what a buyer will experience on the day, the advert becomes a promise you cannot keep.

Clear, factual language travels further than enthusiasm. Claims that require explanation usually signal overreach. Say what the horse does. Avoid describing what it might become.

A buyer can work with limitations that you state plainly. They struggle with surprises. Preparation at this stage means you resist the urge to improve the story. It means you allow the horse to be seen as it is, not as you hope it will be interpreted.

Match claims with evidence

If you describe a horse as consistent, that should be demonstrated. If you describe it as suitable for a discipline, make sure the work supports that claim. If you mention versatility or potential, those words need to be framed carefully and honestly. Capability must be shown, not implied.

Buyer doubt is difficult to recover from once created.

Managing the assessment

A buyer does not need to see everything. They need to see enough to make an informed decision. Your role is to structure the assessment so the horse can be understood without pressure or theatre.

Keep demonstrations simple. Dress the part. Decide in advance what the horse will and will not be asked to do. Know where your boundaries sit. When you hold those boundaries, you protect both the horse and the integrity of the sale Consistency matters more than spectacle.

Preparing yourself

Preparation is not limited to the horse. It includes knowing your answers before the questions are asked. Understand the horse's history. Be clear about strengths, limitations, and past issues. Deciding what will be disclosed verbally and what will be confirmed in writing.

It means you are organised. Records available. Details accurate. No searching for paperwork while a buyer waits.

It also means being steady. Buyers take their cues from you. If you are rushed, defensive, or uncertain, confidence drops quickly. Calm, consistent communication does more than persuasion ever will.

Timing and judgement

Sometimes preparation reveals that you should not proceed yet. If the story you are telling feels forced, if key information is missing, or if you find yourself explaining away gaps, that tells you something.

Time rarely harms a sound sale but pressure often does.

Respect in practice

How you frame and present the horse is an act of respect. Respect for the horse, who deserves to be assessed as it truly is, respect for the buyer, who deserves clarity, and respect for yourself. You should not be placed in the position of defending something you knew was not quite accurate.

When you prepare the sale properly, very little needs to be managed. The advert matches the horse. The conversation matches the advert. And the decision becomes straightforward.

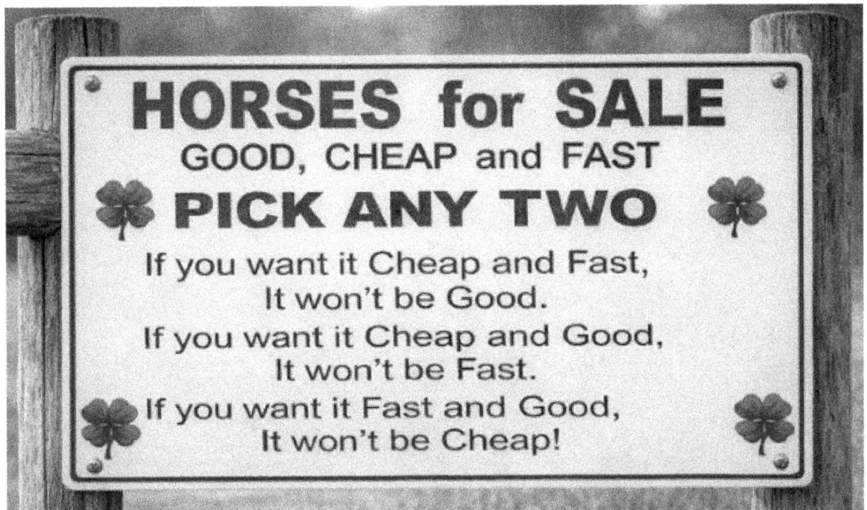

Shaping expectations

The aged mare

We gave away an aged broodmare as a companion and occasional riding horse. She was a firm favourite of ours. About a month later, the new owner rang to say she could no longer keep her, having lost their rental property. We took the mare back and quickly found another home.

Around ten days later, the original people rang again, distressed and pleading to have her back, as they missed her terribly. By then, returning the mare would have disrupted a home where she had already settled and require us to withdraw her from people who had acted in good faith (even if they agreed).

We declined. A horse is not something to be moved back and forth as circumstances change.

Once responsibility is transferred, it must be honoured.

Good professional photos can make the difference between a good sale or no sale.

Chapter 6

Pricing fairly

Market reality, value, and avoiding costly mistakes

Pricing a horse is often treated as a technical exercise, as though the right number can be derived if you look hard enough at the market. You compare recent sales, listen to opinions, adjust for breeding, training, and presentation, and then settle on a figure you feel comfortable with.

In reality, price does far more than reflect value. It signals your intent.

Before a buyer sees your horse, the price has already shaped their expectations. It tells them how you see the horse, how confident you are in its suitability, and how much negotiation you expect. Buyers may not articulate this consciously, but they respond to it all the same.

This is why pricing can either support the sale quietly or undermine it before it begins.

Why listing a price matters

If you do not list a price, you create barriers for buyers before any conversation begins. A buyer may assume that a horse without a stated price is beyond their reach and simply move on. particularly those who are time poor or cautious of awkward enquiries. Others may feel that asking for a price places them at a disadvantage or opens the door to negotiation they are not prepared for.

Buyers want to assess suitability and affordability at the same time. When one of those pieces is missing, they are less likely to invest energy in the process. Phrases such as "price on application" or vague references to value, often have the same effect.

While some sellers hope that withholding a price encourages dialogue, it often has the opposite effect, filtering out serious, suitable buyers who do not want to waste time pursuing a horse that may never have been financially realistic for them in the first place.

What is my horse actually worth?

"A horse is only worth what someone is prepared to pay for it." This truism can be hard to accept.

- Not what it cost you to breed or buy.
- Not how many years you have invested in its education.
- Not how carefully you have raised it.
- And not how strongly you would like to make a profit.

Those factors matter deeply to *you*. They may even be entirely justified. But they *do not determine market value*.

Buyers assess worth through different criteria. They are weighing suitability, risk, confidence, and future cost. If your evaluation does not align with how buyers see your horse, you will rarely achieve a higher price.

If you hold a horse too long at an unrealistic price, it does not stand still. It ages. It may lose fitness. It may injure itself. Circumstances change. A horse that could have sold well can become harder to place through no fault of its own.

A price that reflects buyer perception gives the sale momentum. A price that reflects only your history with the horse can quietly stall the sale.

Separate your personal investment from market reality.

Some sellers price a horse slightly higher expecting negotiation to follow. Personally, I don't do this. Once I have decided on a price, I stand firm, because that is what I want to sell it for.

Under-pricing carries its own risks. If you price your horse well below its peers, you may attract attention quickly, but not always the right kind. Urgency increases. Pressure mounts. Buyers with limited experience or unrealistic expectations rush in, and sellers are tempted to move quickly rather than carefully.

Accurate pricing sits between these extremes. It reflects what the horse can do now, not its potential. It acknowledges both strengths and limitations. It acknowledges the buyer's risk as well as the seller's investment. It is important to listen more than you speak.

Fair pricing positions the horse so the right buyer can act while the opportunity is still intact.

Using market research to price realistically

Pricing fairly does not mean you price blindly.

Market research anchors your pricing, because buyers are making comparisons whether you acknowledge it or not. It helps you understand where your horse sits in relation to others currently available, and how buyers at different experience levels interpret value.

When researching price, you are not just looking at horses. You are examining *outcomes*. Specifically:

- Which horses are actually selling?
- At what level?
- To which type of buyer?
- how long they are staying on the market?

Unsold adverts tell a story too. Useful sources include:

- Current online sale platforms and classifieds
- Breed society listings and newsletters
- Discipline-specific sale pages
- Sale catalogues and recent auction results
- Conversations with trainers, breeders, and professionals who see volume

Make sure you check *sale prices rather than asking prices*. These reflect reality.

Who and how to ask

- Trainers who regularly match horses with riders
- Breeders selling similar stock
- Coaches working with buyers at your target level
- Sale agents or auctioneers

When you ask others for their perspective, avoid framing the question as "What should I charge?" Instead, ask:

- What sort of buyers are active right now for this type of horse
- What are they prioritising?

- What price range are they comfortable with for a horse at this stage?
- What factors would increase or reduce interest?
- How does my horse compare in age, education, and temperament to others currently for sale?
- Is this horse suitable for a novice, amateur, or experienced rider?
- Does the price reflect proven ability or future potential?
- Is the discipline or purpose clearly defined, or implied?
- How quickly do I realistically need to sell? Urgency does not change value, but it might change strategy.

Understanding buyer experience levels

Price means different things to different buyers.

Less experienced buyers may associate higher price with safety and reliability. More experienced buyers assess price against training, soundness, and opportunity cost.

If your horse is best suited to a particular buyer group, the price should make sense *to that group*. Pricing outside their expectations can quietly exclude them.

Positive factors that influence price

Some strengths are recognised by the market more readily than others, provided they are presented accurately and without exaggeration.

These include:

- **Pedigree and breeding**, particularly where bloodlines are known, and proven in the discipline for which the horse is being offered
- **Breed, sex and height,** where it aligns with buyer demand
- **Age** in relation to current education and longevity of use
- **Usefulness**, meaning what the horse can reliably do now.
- Whether the horse is a specialist or an all-rounder, and at what level.
- **Temperament and manners**, both under saddle and on the ground.
- **Level and quality of training**, not just time spent in work.

- Is the rider/trainer/breeder/owner well known and highly regarded?
- **Performance of siblings or close relatives**, where comparable
- a genuine competition record that justifies the price

Each of these can support a higher price when a buyer sees these as 'needs'. None justify a higher price on their own.

Pedigree does not override temperament. Training does not replace suitability. A good sibling record does not guarantee individual ability.

Understanding the market

Market conditions can slow sales. The more urgently you wish to sell, the more you must "meet the market."

Markets are governed by factors out of your control, such as drought, widespread flooding, and poor economic conditions. In a "hot" market, prices rise due to optimism, rare breeding/breed, an Olympic games year, high cattle prices, and the like.

Both ends of the market are not sustainable, but may easily impact prices you can expect in the short term.

When price is not the primary driver

Occasionally, money is not the central consideration. This may be because the horse has limited use, is no longer rideable, or because *placement matters more than return*.

“Free to good home” is frequently misunderstood. Despite good intentions, it often attracts the highest risk enquiries unless boundaries are stated clearly from the outset.

If you offer a horse without charge, it still carries value. That value shifts from financial to ethical.

It is reasonable to state that:

- The horse is free subject to suitability
- References will be required
- The seller reserves the right to refuse without explanation
- A contract will still apply

Flexibility without confusion

Make sure you inform the buyer if the price is inclusive, or exclusive of taxes. Clear wording allows buyers to assess suitability and affordability together, such as:

- "Priced at X including GST"
- "Priced at X, reflecting age and training"
- "Open to discussion with the right home"
- "Expected price range X to Y"

Avoid language such as "make an offer," "no time wasters" or "no photo collectors". These words just clutter your advert and tend to discourage the very buyers you want.

Effectively all enquirers are "time-wasters" except for the one who buys.

Pricing reflection checklist

Look at your horse today. Ask yourself:

- What can the horse do consistently now
- What level of rider does it genuinely suit
- What management does it require to stay sound, comfortable and reliable

The market context

- What comparable horses are actually selling for, not just advertised at
- How quickly are similar horses moving on
- Whether demand in this category is narrow or broad

Your position. Be honest about:

- Whether you are selling by choice or necessity
- How much time you realistically have

If the price you have in mind feels difficult to justify calmly, it is worth revisiting. Not because you must lower it, but because uncertainty here tends to echo through the rest of the sale.

Unexpected situations

A buyer may enquire about one horse, and you may suggest another that is more suitable. Or they may want to pursue a different horse, even if you had no intention of selling it.

You must be firm about what price you would accept, or be prepared to say "no" politely.

You can invite a reasonable offer and consider whether it exceeds your expectations, provided you are comfortable with the suitability. This is where negotiation can play a role in confirming seriousness.

Never let bargaining override your reservations about the match.

Fair pricing does not guarantee an easy process. It does remove one of the most common sources of friction however. It allows conversations to focus on suitability rather than negotiation.

It signals that you understand both your horse and the market it sits within, and it gives the right buyer confidence to step forward while the opportunity is there.

Seek guidance

Most people do not sell enough horses to become skilled at selling.

A breeder may sell a handful each year. An owner may sell only once or twice in a lifetime. Unlike professionals who see volume, most sellers are navigating unfamiliar territory while emotionally invested in the outcome.

This matters.

Limited experience can lead you to overvalue effort, underestimate buyer perception, or misread market signals. None of this reflects poor intent. It reflects lack of exposure.

Recognising this learning curve allows you to reflect, seek perspective, and avoid making decisions based on a single past experience or one current outcome.

Selling well is a learned skill. Seeking guidance is not weakness. It is stewardship.

Seek guidance if you are unsure.

When dropping the price isn't the answer

A common moment for sellers comes when the enquiries slow down and doubt creeps in. The instinct is often to assume the price is the problem, and to reduce it in the hope that interest will suddenly increase.

In reality, dropping the price rarely solves the underlying issue.

Most times, the seller will realise that reducing the price did not attract more suitable buyers. Instead, it shifted the type of enquiry. Serious buyers were not reassured. They became cautious.

Meanwhile, bargain-focused enquiries increased, often from people who were not well placed to take the horse on.

The problem was not the price.

The horse was well priced for the right buyer, but the advert was not clearly speaking to that buyer's needs. Lowering the price created noise, not clarity.

What is learned

- Price signals value and suitability, not just affordability
- Dropping the price can undermine confidence rather than build it
- The right buyer is looking for fit, not a discount
- Clarity in advertising matters more than price adjustment

Related reading

"Maybe I should drop the price..."

https://jeanettegower.substack.com/p/maybe-i-should-drop-the-price?utm_source=chatgpt.com

Chapter 7

Advertising successfully

Attracting the right interest

Most sellers treat an advertisement as a starting point, something you write quickly so the process can begin. In reality, an advertisement is rarely the beginning of anything. It is the continuation of a conversation that has already been taking place quietly in the buyer's mind.

By the time a buyer reads an advert, they are not looking for persuasion. They are looking for confirmation. Confirmation that this horse falls within what they are willing to consider. Confirmation that the seller understands the horse. Confirmation that engaging further will not waste their time.

This is why advertising is not about saying more. It is about stating the right things clearly enough that the right buyer recognises themselves and the wrong one moves on.

A good advertisement does not try to make a horse appealing to everyone. It creates a narrow, accurate doorway and invites buyers to decide for themselves whether to step through it.

This is where preparation truly matters.

Make sure you plan your advert well ahead of the closing date and *always, always time it for when you are free to answer queries.*

There is nothing more frustrating for a buyer than not being able to reach you!

Advertising does not exist in isolation. For many buyers, particularly experienced ones, an advert is not the first time they have encountered you or your horses. It is simply the moment at which interest becomes active.

Exposure outside of formal advertising matters more than most sellers recognise.

Buyers notice who appears consistently, who turns up at competitions, shows, clinics, or training days. Who is quietly involved, maybe not performing, but present. They notice who seems connected to the horse community in a grounded way and who appears only when something is for sale.

A seller who is seen regularly, whether through a Facebook page, a small website, local events, or simply word of mouth, feels less risky to approach. Buyers feel as though they already know something about you, even if they have never spoken to you directly.

Networking in this context does not require strategy or polish. It often looks like ordinary participation. Riding at a local show. Attending clinics. Helping out. Talking to people. Letting others see how you handle horses, how you speak about them, and how you conduct yourself when nothing is being sold.

These interactions build quietly. In fact, it may be enough to sell your horse before you even advertise it.

When buyers encounter your advertisement, it feels different. It is no longer just words on a page. It is connected to a person they have seen, heard about, or watched over time.

This matters whether you are selling one horse or many.

Advertising sets expectations. This is where many sales quietly unravel. Buyers arrive expecting the horse described, and instead meet a version that is different from the description implied.

The role of photographs

Advertisements without photos are increasingly ignored. In a crowded online market, buyers rarely invest time in listings that give them nothing visual to assess.

Buyers assume a reason, and it is rarely positive. Simple, clear images are better than none.

If a buyer asks for current photos and you cannot supply them, you will likely find the buyer will move on.

Photographs do far more than show what your horse looks like. They signal care, professionalism, and intent long before a buyer has read a single word.

Poor photos do not just fail to help. They actively undermine confidence. Good photos do not need to be dramatic, just realistic and current.

A clear, well-taken photograph communicates more than any description. Australian Stock Horse colt, Chalani Star Wars. Photo: Janice de Gennaro.

Blurry images, cluttered backgrounds, unbalanced horses, or unflattering angles suggest haste or indifference, even when that is not your intention.

Buyers notice litter in the background. They notice muddy legs, poorly fitted tack, and horses standing awkwardly because no time was taken to present them properly.

Show the horse in a good light, standing correctly on level ground, with the whole body visible. One clear side-on image is often more valuable than five poorly framed alternatives.

Where appropriate, an action shot can help buyers understand movement and way of going, but it should support the description rather than replace it.

As the value of the horse increases, expectations rise.

For higher value horses, professional photography becomes essential. Use photos taken at discipline specific competitions, or accepting awards. They are often your horse's best moments and can make your advert stand out instantly. Important: Watermarked photos cannot legally be used. If you haven't purchased the image, or don't have written permission from the photographer, don't use it.

At home or a neutral venue, set up a photo shoot with someone experienced who has a good camera. Have another person to get ears pricked for stand up (conformation) shots, and allow at least an hour.

Always think about the space where you will take the photos, and make sure the background is contrasting or distant.

You can do free movement in an arena or lunge area, or set up a ridden shoot showing what your horse can do. Take video on your camera at the same time.

Photos should show the horse clearly enough that the right buyer feels confident taking the next step.

This usually includes having extra photos to pass on after the first enquiry, such as legs, headshots and anything not shown in the advertisment.

Buyers may interpret the absence of quality imagery as a mismatch. At that end of the market, photographs are evidence.

A good photograph tells a buyer that you care and often increases its perceived value.

Advertising as an individual versus a program

How you approach advertising should reflect who you are and how often you sell.

A private owner selling a single horse does not need the same level of visibility as a breeder with young stock each year, or a trainer regularly selling horses on behalf of clients. What matters is consistency rather than scale.

For someone selling one horse, free or low cost channels may be entirely sufficient. Clear adverts, supported by good photos, honest communication, combined with quiet participation in the community, will reach the right buyers more effectively than broad but unfocused exposure.

I go into depth about recognising and taking your own good photographs in my book *The Thinking Horse Breeder.*

Available from Amazon.

If you sell horses regularly, more structure becomes useful. A simple website, a consistent social media presence, or regular updates about horses in work allows buyers to follow along over time. This builds familiarity and trust before a specific horse is even advertised.

The key difference is not money spent. It is continuity.

Paid advertising or free promotion?

Paying for advertising is not inherently better. Paid platforms can increase reach, particularly for higher value horses or niche markets, but they do not replace credibility. A poorly presented advert seen by more people simply creates more confusion or disinterest.

Free promotion, when done well, is often more effective. Clear, accurate advertising combined with consistent presence builds far more trust than paid reach alone. Clear social media posts. Thoughtful updates. Sharing progress without hype. These allow buyers to observe without pressure.

Quiet consistency builds trust

Many sellers underestimate how much buyers value predictability. A Facebook page that is updated occasionally but consistently. A website that is simple but accurate. A steady presence at events rather than a sudden burst of activity. These things signal reliability far more strongly than polished marketing ever could.

Buyers are looking for signs that engaging with you will feel straightforward and safe.

This is part of the same groundwork discussed earlier. It is not about attracting attention. It is about reducing uncertainty.

By the time a buyer reads your advert, the decision to enquire has often already been influenced by everything they have noticed beforehand, even if they cannot articulate it clearly. It is the visible tip of a much longer process.

Advertising, then, is not a single act.

Where you advertise and why it matters

Where you advertise your horse shapes buyer expectations just as strongly as how you advertise it. Where you advertise depends on the type of horse and the buyer you are trying to reach.

Different platforms carry different assumptions about risk, vetting, support, and suitability. Buyers interpret the location of an advert before they interpret its content. Certain buyers will regularly search Magazines, while others will search Facebook or Marketplace.

Some advertising fees are expensive, but often come with discounts if you buy a package. Some mediums will design a quality advertisement on your behalf.

Advertising on a general marketplace suggests accessibility and volume. Advertising through a trainer or breeder suggests filtering and context. Advertising at auction signals opportunity paired with increased responsibility for the buyer. A poster on a local noticeboard suggests that the horse is known locally or selling is not urgent.

None of these pathways are inherently better than another. Problems arise when sellers rely on the platform to fill in the gaps for them

- A private advertisement still needs clarity.
- An auction listing still requires honesty.
- A professional referral still needs transparency.

Many buyers now search across multiple platforms simultaneously. Use multiple platforms where appropriate, but keep your message consistent across all of them.

Instead of asking where buyers look, ask where your ideal buyer is most likely to be, and what assumptions they will bring with them.

What must be included in every advertisement

This information is non negotiable. It should be stated clearly without embellishment.

- Heading to grab attention
- Location of the horse
- Contact details for the seller or agent
- Height, age, and sex
- Breed or breeding if known
- Current level of training or use
- Rider suitability stated accurately
- Price or a clear price range

What should be described rather than labelled

Certain aspects of a horse are better explained than summarised.

Rather than relying on shorthand, describe:

- How the horse behaves in new environments
- How it responds to pressure or mistakes
- What kind of routine it thrives in
- What level of consistency it requires from the rider

This allows buyers to interpret suitability through their own experience rather than trying to decode vague terms.

Heading

A good heading helps the right buyer to keep reading. It does quiet but important work. It is there to orientate the buyer quickly and accurately.

A strong heading allows a reader to decide, within seconds, whether the horse is likely to be relevant to them. Straightforward headings tend to perform better than clever ones, particularly in a crowded marketplace where buyers are scanning rather than reading closely.

A heading that reflects your horse's type, purpose, or suitability builds trust early. A vague, long winded, or overly promotional heading may attract attention, but often the wrong kind.

If the heading could apply to almost any horse, it is probably too vague. If it allows the wrong buyer to imagine themselves in the picture, it is not doing its job. If a headline could sit comfortably on a sale board, catalogue entry, or website tile without explanation, it's probably doing the job. If it needs punctuation or persuasion, it's likely doing too much.

Method of sale

State your method of sale clearly. The language you use around price and process sets the emotional tone of the sale. It reduces false assumptions.

Buyers read these phrases carefully. They are listening for flexibility, firmness, urgency, or competition. When sellers use them casually or inconsistently, misunderstandings arise long before a conversation begins.

Common sale terms:

Price negotiable

Buyers interpret this as an invitation to discuss value, not necessarily to offer less. It attracts people who want conversation and flexibility. It can also invite low offers if not paired with confidence.

Best used when you are open to discussion but clear about your expectations.

ONO (or near offer)

This signals a willingness to negotiate, often around a reasonably firm price. Buyers hear this as "some movement possible, but not unlimited."

Best used when the price is realistic and you are open to sensible discussion.

Best price or best offer

This creates a competitive atmosphere. Buyers may feel pressure to offer quickly or higher than asking. It can also deter careful buyers who dislike bidding dynamics.

Best used when demand is expected to be strong and the seller is comfortable managing multiple enquiries.

Expressions of interest

This signals that price and conditions are not fixed and may depend on suitability, timing, or volume of interest. Buyers interpret this as a selective process rather than a straightforward transaction.

Best used for higher value horses, breeding stock, or situations where placement matters as much as price.

First option or first refusal

This suggests priority will be given to a particular buyer or group before the horse is offered more widely. Buyers who are not in that group will often wait rather than compete.

Best used only when this is genuinely the case, and not as a placeholder.

Serious enquiries invited. Price available on request.

For higher value or specialised horses. This wording works best when paired with:

- a clear description of the horse's level and history
- strong imagery and video
- a well defined buyer profile

Without those, it can feel evasive.

Offered by private treaty. Priced at X

For off market sales, this reassures buyers that there is structure and expectation, even if the sale is not public or time bound. The horse is generally offered by word of mouth.

Buyer references required

This signals that suitability matters and that the seller will be selective. It reassures serious buyers and deters those who want to move quickly without scrutiny.

Best used when you are prepared to follow through consistently..

Clear language gives you something solid to return to if a buyer pushes boundaries. You are not changing your position. You are referring back to what was stated from the beginning. When these terms are absent or ambiguous, buyers fill the gaps themselves. One buyer may assume the price is firm. Another may assume it is flexible. One may feel misled when another is prioritised.

Advertising NO NOs that quietly cost credibility

Buyers form impressions quickly. Certain advertising habits immediately reduce trust, even when the horse itself is perfectly acceptable. Avoiding these mistakes matters as much as including the right information.

Clichés instead of description

Phrases such as “stunning”, “one in a million”, “dream horse”, or “confidence giver” mean very little without context. Experienced buyers read past them. Inexperienced buyers may be misled. Describe what the horse does. Let the reader draw their own conclusion.

Overstating conformation

Statements such as “excellent conformation” or “perfect type” invite scrutiny. If the horse truly has strengths, show them through clear photos and accurate description. Make sure you spell conFORMation, not confirmation.

Buyers trust their eyes more than adjectives.

Selling the horse on cuteness alone

“Cute”, “sweet”, or “adorable” are not selling points for a riding horse. They may describe temperament, but they do not replace suitability, training, or soundness. Cuteness does not carry a horse through a difficult transition.

Treating colour as value

Colour is a preference, not a qualification. Unless colour is genuinely rare within the breed and sought after by the target buyer, over-emphasising it signals a lack of substance. Colour should be mentioned, not marketed.

Using words that contradict the photos

When photos do not support the description, buyers disengage immediately. Calling a horse "athletic" when it is poorly muscled, or "stunning" when it is plain, undermines everything else.

A good advert filters quietly without persuading. A buyer feels reassured rather than sold to. When a buyer thinks the horse is suitable, price often fades into the background. In fact the buyer may wonder why the horse is so cheap!

RIVINGTON THE CATS PYJAMAS

Superb Childs Welsh A Gelding
11.3 3/8hh Bay 3yo. Reg WPCS, APSB & SHC.

This wonderful pony has the most fabulous nature and quiet temperament. Broken in by 11yo boy and has been perfect for kids right from the start. Ridden only by children, he is very straightforward and easy.

Soft snaffle mouth, goes kindly on the bit or on a loose rein. Steady, soft paces with a super smooth canter and great brakes. PJ will be an excellent First Ridden and Leading Rein Show Hunter pony, as well as an ideal pony club, dressage and interschool mount.

PJ is easy to catch, float and clip. He has done obstacle courses, trail rides with little jumps, lake rides, youngstock shows and has started his newcomer ridden year. He has been taught to have a gate opened and shut off him. Saddle up and enjoy a pony that is the same out and about as at home and doesn't require riding every day to maintain him. PJ doesn't care about being left tied to the float or where his mates are when being ridden.

PJ has been afforded the same training as our stock horses and he is just the most delightful loveable character that we have owned since a weanling. Unfortunately my boys are too tall and they have made the decision he's ready for a new little rider.

An excellent sales advert for a child's pony

Chapter 8

Advertising examples

and checklists for you

A good advert opens up a conversation. It does not attempt to conclude it.

It protects your horse from being viewed multiple times by unsuitable buyers, protects you from endless clarification, and allows serious buyers to arrive already orientated.

Advertisement examples matched with buyer psychology

Different buyers read adverts through very different lenses. The same words can reassure one buyer and alarm another. Well written advertisements do not try to neutralise this. They lean into it.

When adverts match buyer psychology, enquiries become fewer but better. Conversations slow down and deepen. And sales, when they happen, tend to hold together.

The following examples show how small changes in wording can significantly alter how a horse is perceived.

They are demonstrations of how an advert can describe reality without over-promising, and how it can filter quietly before anyone books a visit.

Example 1. The schoolmaster or confidence giving horse

Buyer mindset

This buyer is prioritising safety, predictability, and emotional security. They are often returning to riding, rebuilding confidence, or buying for a family member. They are alert to exaggeration and deeply sensitive to surprises. They are not looking for brilliance. They are looking for reassurance.

> **Genuine Schoolmaster**
>
> 12 year old 15.2hh bay gelding, well handled and sensible under saddle.
>
> Ridden consistently by an adult amateur for hacking, lessons, and low level competition. Comfortable alone or in company, sensible in open spaces, and unfazed by normal farm and traffic environments.
>
> Established at walk, trot, and canter with basic lateral work. Not sharp, not spooky, and forgiving of rider mistakes.
>
> Easy to handle on the ground. Loads, ties, clips, and stands for farrier and vet. No known vices.
>
> Best suited to a confident novice or returning rider wanting a genuine, kind horse for pleasure riding and low level activities.
>
> Open to vet check. Located in X. Priced at X.

Why this works

- It does not promise perfection.
- It names what the horse does and does not do.
- It reassures without overselling.
- It filters out ambitious buyers who want more than the horse can offer.

Checklist for this type of advert

Include

☐ Age and height
☐ Rider suitability clearly stated
☐ Behaviour under saddle and on the ground
☐ Environment exposure
☐ Level of education
☐ What the horse is not suited for

Avoid
☐ Competition language that creates false expectations
☐ Vague claims like bombproof or confidence giver without context

Example 2. The young or green horse

Buyer mindset

This buyer expects work, time, and uncertainty. They are not afraid of projects, but they want honesty so they can assess whether the project fits their skill set. They are listening for realism, not reassurance.

Green young horse

4 year old 15.2h QH gelding, lightly started and showing a willing attitude.

Professionally backed and ridden quietly for the past three months. Walk, trot, and canter established in the arena, with basic exposure to trails and new environments.

Still green and learning, but straightforward and sensible for age. No buck, rear, or bolt. Requires a confident, educated rider to continue development.

Good to handle, loads and travels well, and has been easy to manage so far.

Suitable for an experienced rider or professional looking for a young horse to bring on. Not suitable for novices or riders seeking a finished horse.

Open to vet check. Located in X. Priced at X.

Why this works

- It does not confuse green with easy.
- It names the developmental stage clearly.
- It protects inexperienced buyers from making assumptions.

Checklist for this type of advert

Include
☐ Exact stage of training
☐ Time under saddle
☐ Behavioural observations so far
☐ Clear rider requirement

☐ Honest statement about immaturity

Avoid
☐ Phrases like easy young horse without context
☐ Implying readiness the horse does not yet have

Example 3. The competition horse

Buyer mindset

This buyer listens for precision. They care about Breed or Breeding, history, consistency, and evidence. They are not impressed by adjectives without proof. They are evaluating risk and trajectory.

Proven Show Jumping Horse

8 year old 16.1hh Grey Warmblood mare competing consistently at X level.

Established in competition with regular outings over the past two seasons. Competed by an adult amateur under professional guidance, with consistent results.

Correctly educated on the flat, with established lateral work and consistent contact. Jumping X courses comfortably and confidently.

Travels well, settles at competitions, and handles atmosphere without issue.

Best suited to a rider wanting to compete at current level with potential to progress under experienced guidance.

Full competition and veterinary history available. Open to vet check. Located in X. Priced at X.

Why this works

- It grounds ability in history.
- It avoids promising future success.
- It speaks the language of experienced buyers.

Checklist for this type of advert

Include
☐ Current level and consistency
☐ Rider type it has been competing with
☐ Competition exposure and temperament
☐ Honest assessment of potential versus reality

Avoid
☐ Claims of unlimited potential
☐ Hiding limitations behind ambitious language

Example 4. The broodmare or breeding prospect

Buyer mindset

This buyer cares about Breed, genetics, soundness for breeding, and transparency around limitations. They expect clarity and documentation. They are not shopping emotionally.

> **Registered Morgan Broodmare**
>
> 10 year old 15h brown mare offered for breeding purposes only.
>
> Proven producer with X foals on the ground. Easy breeder and good mother.
>
> Non rideable due to previous injury. Full veterinary details, breeding history and documentation available.
>
> Suitable for a breeder seeking a reliable mare with old bloodlines and proven production.
>
> Located in X. Priced at X.

Why this works

- It states purpose clearly.
- It discloses limitations without apology.
- It prevents unsuitable enquiries entirely.

Checklist for this type of advert

Include
☐ Purpose of sale stated upfront
☐ Breeding and registration details
☐ Clear disclosure of non rideability if applicable
☐ Veterinary transparency

Avoid
☐ Ambiguous language that invites riding enquiries
☐ Minimising significant history

Example 5. The hard to place or specialised horse

Buyer mindset

This buyer is rare but valuable. They are experienced, self aware, looking for honesty rather than reassurance. They do not need persuasion. They need specifics.

Talented but Sensitive

Quality black gelding, 16h suited to an experienced, quiet rider.

Athletic and capable, but not tolerant of inconsistent riding or busy environments. Thrives with routine and a confident person with quiet hands.

Not suitable for novices or riders seeking an uncomplicated horse.

In the right hands, offers scope and responsiveness.

Open to discussion with experienced riders who understand this type of horse.

Why this works

- It protects the horse.
- It filters heavily.
- It speaks directly to the right buyer.

Checklist for this type of advert

Include
☐ Clear description of challenges
☐ Explicit rider requirements
☐ Honest explanation of why the horse needs a specific home

Avoid
☐ Trying to make the horse sound easier than it is

Example 6. A child's pony

Buyer mindset

This buyer is usually a parent, sometimes guided by a coach. They want safety and reliability, but they also understand performance. They are alert to exaggeration and wary of ponies described as suitable for beginners when they are not. They are looking for a pony that can carry a capable child confidently, not teach the basics from scratch.

When selling an experienced child's pony, it is common for more than one adult to be involved in the decision. A parent may be focused on safety, longevity, and suitability for the child's current stage. They may also be thinking ahead to whether the pony could suit younger siblings in time.

A coach or mentor, by contrast, is often listening for performance history, scope, and whether the pony will continue to support the child's development without being outgrown too quickly.

Both perspectives are valid, and both usually know the child well.

A well written advert respects this dynamic. It does not try to reassure everyone with the same language. Instead, it separates safety from skill, experience from beginner suitability, and success from universality. This allows parents and coaches to have an informed conversation together, rather than relying on assumptions or filling in gaps themselves.

Experienced, quality child's pony.

Registered Welsh B grey gelding, 13.3hh, child's pony.

Successfully competed at the highest levels in both open hack and breed rings, with multiple championship wins. Consistent, mannerly, and well educated, with extensive experience in show environments.

Enjoys ride outs, Pony Club activities, and obstacle courses. Sensible in open spaces and familiar with busy environments.

Safe for most riders but not suitable for beginners. Best suited to a capable child under adult supervision who wants to continue competing or enjoying a well schooled pony.

Rider outgrown. Open to vet check. Located in X. Priced at X.

Why this works

- It separates experience from beginner suitability
- It acknowledges performance without exaggeration
- It explains the pony's strengths and expectations clearly
- It attracts capable homes while discouraging unsuitable ones

Checklist for this type of advert

Include

☐ Height and breed registration

☐ Competition history stated factually
☐ Rider experience level clearly defined
☐ Activities the pony enjoys
☐ Reason for sale if relevant

Avoid
☐ Describing the pony as beginner safe when it is not
☐ Using competition success to imply universal suitability

A well written advertisement anticipates how different buyers will hear the same information, and it respects those differences rather than trying to smooth them away.

Parents, coaches, experienced riders, and specialists all read with their own priorities in mind. When your language is precise, grounded, and honest, it allows those conversations to happen before anyone arrives to view the horse. Fewer people enquire, but the right people stay.

The goal is not to write more, but to write clearly enough that the right buyer recognises the horse without needing interpretation.

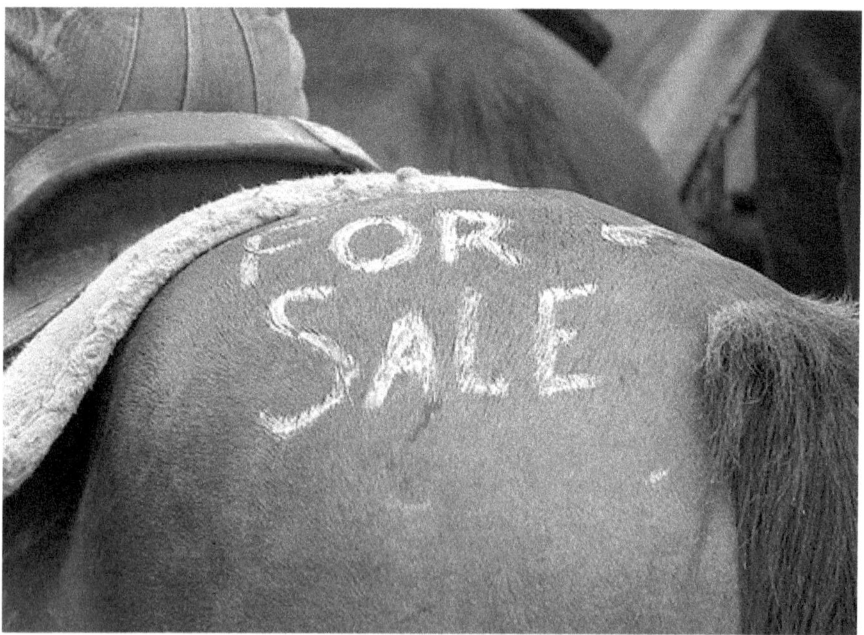

Advertising takes many forms, depending on the market and how urgently you wish to sell.

What does not belong in an advertisement

An advert is not the place for full disclosure of every detail, nor is it the place for statements that could later create legal or practical problems.

Avoid absolute claims about soundness, suitability, or future performance. Avoid language that implies guarantees or outcomes beyond your control. Some information is better discussed once a buyer engages, where context can be provided and questions answered.

Bad advertising examples

Example 1:

A seller advertised a promising dressage horse. The horse was listed at 15.1h but when the buyer inspected the horse, it was barely 14.3h making it unsuitable for official competition. This wasted time for everyone concerned as the buyer had already travelled quite a distance, and the seller had taken the afternoon off work. The buyer left disgruntled.

Key takeaway: always measure a horse before you advertise it.

Example 2:

A seller described a horse as "quiet and suitable for beginners". On arrival, the buyer discovered the horse had only been ridden by experienced riders and had not been exposed to traffic, children, or busy environments. Under saddle the horse was forward and reactive, not dangerous, but clearly green and sensitive. The description had set the wrong expectation. The buyer lost confidence and declined to proceed.

Key takeaway: Nothing was technically wrong with the horse. The wording was.

Example 3:

A seller posted several beautiful photos taken years earlier, when the horse was in regular work and peak condition. By the time the buyer arrived, the horse had been out of work for months and was unfit and heavier. The difference was obvious.

The buyer felt misled before the conversation had even started. Trust, once lost, is hard to recover, and the visit ended quickly.

Key takeaway: Old photos might attract enquiries, but they rarely survive inspection.

Example 4.

A seller wrote an advertisement full of vague praise but very little detail. "Lovely temperament", "great movement", "good home only". No workload, no clear strengths or limitations. Interested buyers had to message back and forth for basic information. Most did not bother.

Serious buyers moved on to clearer listings, and the horse sat unsold for months, not because it lacked quality, but because the advert required too much guesswork.

Key takeaway: Confusion is the enemy of confidence.

Marketing before marketing was called 'Marketing'

Long before online platforms, horses were sold through reputation, consistency, and visibility. This reflection looks back at a time when advertising was slower, quieter, and far more personal.

What stands out is not nostalgia, but principle.

Horses sold because people knew who had them, how they were raised, and what standards sat behind the name. Enquiries came from observation over time, not impulse clicks.

Modern platforms have changed the mechanics, but not the fundamentals. Visibility still matters. Reputation still travels. And buyers still pay attention long before they enquire.

What was learned

- Advertising starts long before an advert is written
- Familiarity builds trust more effectively than novelty
- Consistent presence matters more than loud promotion
- Sellers are always advertising, whether they realise it or not

Related reading

"How we marketed in the good old days"

https://jeanettegower.substack.com/p/how-we-marketed-in-the-good-old-days?utm_source=chatgpt.com

Chapter 9

First contact and follow up

Requests for more information

The first real interaction between buyer and seller often feels deceptively casual. A message. A phone call. A request for more information. On the surface, it appears informal, even friendly. Underneath, however, expectations are already forming on both sides.

Buyers are deciding whether you feel credible, consistent, and safe to deal with. Sellers are beginning to assess whether the interest in front of them is likely to lead anywhere meaningful. Very little of this is said out loud, yet it shapes everything that follows.

How you respond, what you clarify, and what you do not engage with sets the tone for the entire sale. It is also the point at which sellers often feel pulled into longer explanations than they intended, particularly when they sense a buyer's disappointment or pressure.

Learning how to be clear without being drawn into justification is one of the most important skills in selling horses well.

A buyer making contact is not a promise. It is an expression of interest, nothing more.

Sellers sometimes feel obligated to continue conversations simply because someone has taken the time to enquire. This sense of obligation can lead to over-explaining, negotiating suitability, or entertaining scenarios that do not sit comfortably.

You can pause, reflect or say "no". You are the one in control.

Responding politely does not require you to keep the door open indefinitely.

After an initial enquiry, make reasonable steps to check out the buyer. This can include asking for references or going to their Facebook profile page. I will often see things that make me suspicious of a suitable home, such as horses in poor condition, or alternatively, an excellent page showing care and love.

I also look for suitable facilities, fencing, competition or discipline matches, engagement and comments from others, and look at who their friends are. This may tell me a lot.

I will check out websites, profession or anything else likely to give me information.

When the horse is not suitable.

A difficult moment is realising that a buyer is unlikely to be a good match, particularly when the buyer is enthusiastic or emotionally invested.

The mistake you might make here is explaining too much. Long explanations invite debate. Debate invites pressure. Pressure erodes judgement.

Just be calm, brief, and consistent. For example, stating that you do not believe the horse is suitable for the rider's experience or goals is both truthful and complete. You do not need to justify that assessment. You do not need to soften the message.

Some buyers will be unhappy with this. That discomfort does not mean your decision is wrong.

Being firm is not the same as being unkind.

Presenting the horse in person or on video

Once a buyer engages they may ask for more photos, or a specific video. Ask what they want to see. Be prepared for such requests by having video available, or someone ready to help you take some footage over the next few days.

Presentation should reflect the role the horse is being sold for. For example, a high value show horse should be presented with its show bridle, plaited, hindquarter marks and feet oiled, as if it is ready to step foot in the ring. If you have said the horse is good with obstacles, show that.

How the horse is presented, whether in photos or on video, carries significant weight. First impressions count. Buyers are watching what you choose to show, what you avoid, and how confident you appear in what you are offering.

A horse advertised as steady should be shown doing ordinary things calmly, not pushed into situations that exaggerate ability. A green horse should be shown working within its current level, not stretched to impress. Buyers are adept at spotting when a demonstration has been heavily edited.

A good video shows enough for the buyer to assess whether further interest is warranted. It does not attempt to answer every question or prove future success.

Follow-up may include updates for something more current, such as photos of legs if they weren't included in the advert, video of movement, or under saddle, or even photos of relatives, copies of registrations, and pedigree.

As we have often bought from afar, (sight unseen) I cannot tell you the number of times we have asked for video, but no follow-up video arrived. Perhaps they sold the horse, but it would have been appreciated if we had been advised.

Being "too busy" is no excuse unless you were in a car accident, or dramatically sent to hospital. It is simply disrespectful and leaves a buyer hanging.

Managing multiple buyers ethically

At some point, sellers may find themselves dealing with more than one interested buyer. This can feel flattering, but it also introduces complexity.

There is no universal rule about who should be prioritised.

It is reasonable to give priority to the first serious enquirer, particularly if a viewing is then arranged. It is also reasonable to let other interested parties know that someone is ahead of them.

Transparency here protects everyone.

If you have a viewing scheduled, it is appropriate to say so. If you are not holding the horse, say that clearly. If you are willing to accept the first offer subject to funds clearing, that too should be stated upfront.

Problems arise when sellers try to manage expectations quietly, telling different buyers different versions of the same situation.

Holding a horse and accepting payment

Whether or not you hold a horse between viewings is a personal decision, but it must be communicated clearly.

Some sellers will hold a horse with a deposit. Others will not hold at all. Both positions are acceptable, provided they are stated early and applied consistently.

Accepting a full payment from a buyer before others have viewed the horse is ethically acceptable if that is your stated policy. It is not acceptable if other buyers have been led to believe they have priority.

Buyers will sometimes apply pressure by offering more than the advertised price. This is uncomfortable, but not uncommon. If you are committed to a fair process, it is reasonable to decline escalation and proceed as originally stated.

Changing terms mid process creates resentment.

At some point, sellers may encounter a situation that feels deceptively positive. More than one buyer is interested. Enquiries overlap. One buyer wants to move quickly, while another has a viewing scheduled. Occasionally, someone offers to pay in full before anyone else has even seen the horse. Or perhaps a viewing can't take place until a buyer travels from a distance or can get time off work.

There is no single correct way to handle competing interests. You may well feel overwhelmed and pressured to make a decision you may later regret.

There are, however, consequences to every approach. Below are common approaches, with the implications of each.

Option 1: Giving priority to the first serious enquirer

Some sellers choose to prioritise the first buyer who makes meaningful contact, particularly if a viewing has been arranged.

Why sellers choose this
This approach feels fair and orderly. It respects the time and effort of the first buyer and avoids turning the sale into a race.

Consequences to consider
This can slow the sale if the first buyer is hesitant or ultimately unsuitable. Other buyers may disengage if they feel the process is opaque or drawn out.

When this works best
When the first buyer is clearly suitable for the horse and is actively progressing toward a decision.

Option 2: Allowing viewings in order but not holding the horse

Some sellers allow viewings to proceed in sequence but make it clear that the horse is not held for anyone until a deposit or payment is received.

Why sellers choose this
It keeps momentum and avoids being locked into a single outcome prematurely.

Consequences to consider
Buyers may feel pressure to move quickly, which can be uncomfortable for both cautious and experienced purchasers. This approach requires very clear communication to avoid misunderstandings.

When this works best
When demand is strong and the seller is confident in managing expectations clearly.

Option 3: Holding the horse with a deposit

Some sellers will hold a horse once a deposit is paid, temporarily removing it from the market.

Why sellers choose this
It creates commitment and reduces uncertainty for both parties.

Consequences to consider
Deposits can create emotional and practical complexity if the sale does not proceed. Terms must be clear. Is the deposit refundable? Under what circumstances? For how long is the horse held?

When this works best

When both parties are clear, and prepared to proceed promptly.

Option 4: Accepting full payment before other buyers view

Occasionally, a buyer will offer to pay in full immediately, sometimes even above the advertised price, to secure the horse before others have viewed it.

Why sellers choose this
It removes uncertainty and brings the process to a swift conclusion.

Consequences to consider
This can feel unfair to other buyers if they have been led to believe they would have an opportunity to view. It can also lead to regret if the seller later feels the placement was rushed.

When this works best
When the seller has been explicit from the outset that the horse will be sold to the first buyer who completes payment, and all parties are aware of this policy.

Option 5: Declining escalation and sticking to stated terms

Some sellers choose not to accept higher offers or altered terms once the process is underway.

Why sellers choose this
It preserves integrity and avoids turning the sale into a negotiation contest.

Consequences to consider
You may walk away from a higher price. However, you often preserve goodwill and reduce stress.

When this works best
When suitability and placement matter more to you than maximising price.

The importance of being upfront

Whatever approach you choose, it must be communicated clearly and early. This is especially important if a buyer is travelling from afar. They need to make arrangements such as finding someone to look after their place, book leave, book tickets etc. If you are changing conditions or cancelling the sale because you have found another buyer, advise each party as *soon as possible*, to avoid hard feelings

Letting someone know that another buyer is ahead of them is respectful. So is stating that you will wait until after a scheduled viewing before making decisions. Problems arise when buyers discover these realities indirectly or too late.

If multiple buyers are enquiring at the same time, be clear about where this visit sits in the process.

Multiple enquiries are a positive sign, but they require transparency.

You are not obliged to prioritise the first enquiry, but you are obliged to be honest.

Good practice includes:
• informing buyers when others are viewing
• stating whether the horse is being held or remains available
• explaining your policy on deposits and holds

What matters is that your approach is consistent and stated *upfront*.

Pressure from buyers should not dictate your ethics. A horse is not sold until the money is in your bank account.

Not pending. Not promised. Not shown in a screenshot.

Until funds clear, the horse remains available, regardless of what has been said.

Choosing your position

The right approach is the one you can explain calmly, apply consistently, and stand behind afterwards.

When you communicate clearly, set boundaries early, and resist being pulled into emotional negotiation, most difficult situations resolve themselves. Buyers who are not a good fit fall away. Buyers who are serious lean in.

Scams

Scammers may sound like genuine buyers. They rely on politeness, haste, and assumption. They may send convincing looking screenshots, claim banking delays, or request that the horse be held while funds are "processing". In some cases, they will even encourage you to check your account quickly, knowing that many people glance rather than verify.

Scammers rely on haste and assumption. They may present convincing proof of payment, then reverse or delay it through their bank. Others rely on emotional narratives about their dream horse, urgency, or trust.

Be wary of buyers who rush payment without asking appropriate questions, who offer elaborate stories about forever homes, or who rely heavily on sounding pleasant rather than providing verifiable information.

There is no such thing as a guaranteed forever home. Sounding pleasant is not a safeguard. Professional boundaries are. Selling horses well requires a quiet confidence in the buyer. You do not owe anyone a sale.

When trust and integrity align

Buyer enquiry worksheet

You are not expected to remember every conversation accurately. Good notes protect memory. Patterns emerge over time, not from a single call, but from what repeats, what shifts, and what stays vague.

The following worksheet exists so you don't have to hold everything in your head while also holding everything together. It is not to filter buyers, though it might. It is to prevent overwhelm.

Your checklist should be practical, easy to use when multiple enquiries overlap, and something you refer back to. Assume notes are filled in as information becomes available, not all at once.

Horse:
Advert / Reference:
Date of first contact:
Buyer name:
Best contact method:

1. Intended use
(What the buyer thinks they are buying the horse for)

- Main purpose (e.g. pleasure, competition, confidence, development):

- Discipline or activities mentioned:

- Short-term goal:

- Longer-term hope (if stated):

Notes:

2. Who will be riding the horse?
(Establish reality, not aspiration)

- Primary rider:

- Age:

- Riding experience (brief):

- Recent horses ridden:

- Working with a coach/trainer? □ Yes □ No
  If yes, who:

Notes:

3. Management and environment
(Often where mismatches begin)
Where will the horse be kept:

- Agistment type (private / commercial / home):

- Alone or with other horses:

- Expected riding frequency:

- Who provides daily care:

- Is there ready availability of a horse float in an emergency (vet or fire):

Notes:

4. Support and decision-making
(Who actually decides, and who needs to be comfortable)

- Other people involved:
  □ Parent
  □ Partner
  □ Coach
  □ Trainer

- Will they attend the visit? □ Yes □ No

- Who makes the final decision:

Notes:

5. Practical readiness
(Signals seriousness without judgement)

- Looking to buy:
  □ Immediately
  □ Soon
  □ Just exploring

- Budget discussed? □ Yes □ No

- Transport arranged or understood? □ Yes □ No

- Familiar with vet checks? □ Yes □ No

Notes:

6. Questions they asked
(What they focus on tells you a lot)

- Key questions raised:

- Areas of concern:

- Anything repeated or avoided:

Notes:

7. Your disclosures so far
(Track what you have already said — this matters later)

- Information provided:

- Limitations discussed:

- Management needs explained:

- Anything deferred to later conversation:

Notes:

8. Gaps to clarify later
(Not everything needs answering immediately)

- Questions to raise at visit:
- Information to explain in person:
- Documents to show later:

Notes:

9. Seller reflection (private)
(This is not judgement — it's awareness)

- Initial sense of fit:
  □ Good
  □ Unclear
  □ Likely mismatch
- Pace feels:
  □ Calm
  □ Rushed
  □ Vague
- Anything giving you pause:

Notes:

Download a Fillable PDF of the checklist here: https://jeanettegower.gumroad.com/l/dhihcf

Use code SELLYOURHORSE to get it for free

Chapter 10

Buyer psychology

What shapes decisions more than we realise

When you sell a horse, you are "in the horse business!"

By the time a buyer enquires about your horse, they are already carrying a history with them. That history shapes what they hear, what they trust, what they fear, and how quickly they are willing to move forward. Two buyers can stand in the same place, hear the same words, and walk away with entirely different conclusions.

Understanding buyer psychology allows you to recognise different nuances so that conversations reflect an awareness of their position.

Reading the buyer is as important as presenting the horse.

Buyers do not all listen for the same things. Every buyer arrives with a different filter.

Some are listening for reassurance. Others for precision. Some want warmth and conversation. Others want facts, space, and time to think.

Trouble begins if you assume there is a single buyer mindset and speak to everyone the same way.

A calm, capable seller adjusts without changing their integrity. They do not oversell to nervous buyers, or overexplain to experienced ones. They allow the buyer to reveal themselves, then meet them where they are.

Riding experience and buying experience are not the same

One of the most common misunderstandings in horse sales is assuming that riding ability equals buying confidence.

An experienced rider may still be an inexperienced buyer. They may have ridden many horses, but bought very few. They may be uncertain about vetting, contracts, pricing, or recognising red flags. These buyers often ask cautious questions, double-check information, or seek reassurance not because they lack skill, but because they lack exposure to the buying process itself.

Conversely, an inexperienced rider may be a very experienced buyer. They may have purchased horses before, managed outcomes, and learned hard lessons. They may be decisive, quiet, and less emotionally reactive than expected.

Understanding this distinction helps you respond appropriately, rather than misreading hesitation as disinterest or confidence as carelessness.

Inexperienced buyers: caution, overwhelm and reassurance

Inexperienced buyers often carry more anxiety than they admit.

They may not know which questions to ask, or how to interpret the answers. Many have heard stories of horses being misrepresented, or have had a disappointing experience themselves. Some have been taken for a ride and are now highly alert to anything that feels unclear or rushed.

These buyers benefit from a slower pace. They often appreciate:

- A calm, welcoming environment
- Time to talk before seeing the horse
- Clear explanations without jargon
- Space to reflect rather than being pushed to decide

For these buyers, pressure is counterproductive. Urgency feels unsafe. Silence after a visit may not mean rejection. It may mean they are processing, seeking advice, or trying to reconcile emotion with reason.

By giving them a little more time you often build trust rather than lose momentum.

Experienced buyers: efficiency and space

Experienced buyers tend to move differently.

They often want fewer words, not more. They may not want coffee or extended conversation. They are usually comfortable forming their own judgement and do not need reassurance layered over facts.

This is not rudeness. It is business, emotional economy. These buyers are listening for:

- Consistency in description
- Alignment between words, presentation, and reality
- Calm responses to direct or difficult questions

They may ask fewer questions, but those questions carry weight. They value space to observe and think. Overselling, enthusiasm, or unnecessary explanation can create doubt where none existed.

A seller who allows quiet assessment often earns more respect than one who fills every silence.

Professional buyers: decisiveness without ceremony

Professional buyers often sit in a category of their own. They usually know exactly what they are looking for, and exactly what they are willing to compromise on. They are rarely interested in emotional narratives, apologies, or backstory unless it affects the horse's suitability.

They do not need to be convinced. They need access, accuracy, and boundaries.

Trying to engage a professional buyer with warmth-heavy conversation can feel mismatched. Respect their directness, while remaining transparent and grounded.

Buyers with bad or traumatic past experiences

Some buyers are shaped by what went wrong before.

They may have bought a horse that was unsuitable, unsound, or misrepresented. They may have trusted someone they should not have. These experiences often leave buyers vigilant, sceptical, or slow to commit for their self-protection.

These buyers may:

- Ask very specific questions
- Revisit the same topic more than once
- Request time, second opinions, or vet checks early
- Appear guarded or emotionally distant

The worst response is defensiveness. The best response is steadiness. Consistency over time rebuilds trust more effectively than reassurance in the moment. Clear answers given calmly, without pressure or irritation, allow these buyers to decide when they are ready.

Impulse buyers and fear of missing out

Some buyers are impulsive. Others are driven by fear of missing out. These are two sides of the same coin.

They may want to move quickly, skip steps, or secure the horse before fully assessing suitability. This can feel flattering, but it carries risk for the horse. Sellers should be cautious when:

- Decisions are rushed without reflection
- Questions are avoided rather than explored
- Emotional language replaces practical assessment

Slowing the process protects everyone.

A buyer who is encouraged to pause, think, and confirm their decision is less likely to regret it later. Sellers who hold firm to process, even when enthusiasm is high, reduce the chance of fallout.

Selling sight unseen

Sight unseen purchases usually occur at the higher end of the market, where buyers are accustomed to adding travel costs, vetting expenses, and logistical planning. These buyers rely heavily on:

- Accurate, well-structured video
- Honest description of temperament and management
- Independent veterinary assessment

The seller's responsibility increases when the buyer cannot attend in person. Good video should show:

- The horse in regular work
- Transitions, rhythm, and way of going
- Handling on the ground, including standing and trotting out
- Environment and routine

Some sellers choose to offer practical incentives, such as contributing to travel or delivering the horse to an agreed location. It is a strategic decision that can support goodwill and help the sale proceed.

Third parties: parents, coaches, and mentors

Many buyers do not decide alone. Parents, coaches, mentors, or trusted friends are often involved, particularly with children's horses or performance prospects.

Each brings a different lens.

Parents tend to prioritise safety, longevity, and manageability. Coaches often focus on ability, scope, and progression. Both perspectives are usually informed and valid.

Respecting this dynamic strengthens the process.

What this means for sellers:

Buyers listen not just to what you say, but to how responsibility is held. They notice whether explanations remain consistent, whether boundaries stay steady, and whether pressure is applied when uncertainty appears.

Sellers who are clear, fair, and patient find that buyers ask better questions and make more durable decisions. When that happens, the sale feels smooth and uneventful.

And in horse sales, this is what lasts.

Disclosure or transparency in sales

There is a point in many sales where conversation deepens and the urge to say more increases. The buyer is engaged. Trust feels established. Questions become more specific. Sellers often want to reassure, to be helpful, to demonstrate openness.

But transparency is not the same as saying everything, all at once, without judgement. What you share, when you share it, and how you frame it matters as much as honesty itself.

Sellers who front-load every detail often overwhelm or confuse buyers. Sellers who withhold essential information create resentment later. Neither builds confidence.

Buyers do not need to know everything immediately. They need to know what materially affects suitability and risk.

Information that changes how a horse should be ridden, managed, or placed belongs early. Details requiring explanation or context are best discussed once a buyer is seriously assessing the horse.

Timing matters.

- An advert opens the door.

- First contact sets expectations.
- Deeper disclosure belongs later, when there is space for nuance.

One of the most common missteps is making absolute statements too early, particularly in writing. Claims about soundness, suitability, or future performance may feel reassuring in the moment, but they create risk later. Describing what a horse does is different from guaranteeing what it will always do.

A horse can be sound today and fail a vet check tomorrow. A horse may suit one rider and not another. A horse may cope well within one routine and struggle outside it.

Some discussions are better had verbally, where tone and explanation matter. Written communication is permanent. Once something is written, it can be read without you present and stripped of nuance. It can be used against you in the event of a dispute.

Veterinary history is a common example. If a horse has previously failed a vet check, that information matters and should not be concealed. But it should not be dropped into an early message without explanation. Buyers deserve to understand what failed, when, why, and whether it remains relevant.

That conversation belongs when a buyer is actively assessing, not browsing.

The same applies to management needs, past injuries, or limitations. Transparency does not require loading the buyer with every difficulty. It requires ensuring that nothing material is hidden once an enquiry becomes serious.

One final caution: explaining a situation by criticising trainers, veterinarians, breeders, or previous riders rarely reassures buyers. Shifting blame draws attention away from the horse and onto judgement, and can be quite off-putting to a buyer.

Good disclosure is not about saying more.

It is about saying what is relevant, what matters, at the right time, and standing by it consistently. When you approach communication this way, buyers tend to respond in kind. They ask better questions. They accept limitations more readily. They respect your honesty.

Swap wanted

From Sam: I was selling a pony and getting out of horses due to family circumstances. The buyer wanted to trade for a Shetland pony!

When transparency becomes a moving target

As expectations around disclosure increase, sellers can feel trapped between saying too much and not enough.

This article reflects on the growing complexity of selling horses in an environment where vet checks, records, and retrospective judgement are common.

Some details need discussion, not documentation.

What was learned

- Transparency does not mean unlimited disclosure
- Context matters as much as content
- Writing everything down can create unintended consequences
- Thoughtful conversation protects everyone better than oversharing

Related reading

"Selling a horse may soon become impossible"

https://jeanettegower.substack.com/p/selling-a-horse-may-soon-become-impossible?utm_source=chatgpt.com

Poor buying decisions rarely begin at the point of sale

This reflection explores how poor outcomes are often set in motion well before a horse changes hands. Buyers arrive with assumptions, blind spots, and emotional drivers that shape how they hear what sellers say.

The seller may do everything right, yet still feel uneasy when a buyer ignores clear signals or overestimates their ability to manage the horse in front of them.

The lesson here is about recognising that not every buyer hears caution as caution.

What was learned

- Buyers filter information through their own hopes and fears
- Clear language does not guarantee clear understanding
- Sellers are not responsible for managing buyer ambition
- Saying less can sometimes communicate more

Related reading

"A good old-fashioned rant about bad horse-buying decisions"

https://jeanettegower.substack.com/p/a-good-old-fashioned-rant-about-bad?utm_source=chatgpt.com

Chapter 11

Ethics in selling

The moments that define your standards

Not every decision in selling a horse presents itself as obviously right or wrong.

Most sellers are not choosing between honesty and dishonesty. They are navigating the space in between. A horse that is mostly sound but occasionally uneven. A horse that copes well in familiar hands but tightens under pressure. A management requirement that disappears when handled correctly, yet becomes significant when neglected.

These are the grey areas.

They are rarely dramatic. They are subtle, and that is why they matter.

The horse that is "mostly fine"

A horse that comes in slightly uneven after hard work but trots sound the next day. A horse that needs regular injections to stay comfortable. A horse that objects occasionally, but only with a rider who lacks balance. None of these automatically disqualify a sale.

Add to that the horse who shies violently under unusual circumstances, yet appears steady in routine environments. The horse who will not leave other horses without planting or spinning. The one who becomes anxious if kept alone. The horse who loads reliably at home but resists at competitions. The gelding who is perfect in work but aggressive over feed. The mare who is calm most of the time, yet unpredictable when in season.

Each of these horses may be mostly fine. The issue is not the existence of imperfection. The issue is whether the buyer understands the pattern.

It is tempting to describe these matters as minor. It is easy to say, "He has never done that before," or "She is only like that in certain situations." Sometimes that is accurate. Sometimes it is selective memory protecting you from discomfort.

If you know a behaviour appears under specific conditions, say so. If you know soundness depends on careful management, explain it. If the horse needs company to remain settled, disclose that. If it reacts strongly to traffic, dogs, machinery, or separation, mention it before it becomes someone else's problem.

You do not need to dramatise flaws. You can simply describe what you know.

Management that only works in the right hands

Many horses are manageable because you manage them well.

You know how much feed they tolerate before becoming sharp. You know they must be ridden consistently to remain relaxed. You know they cannot be left spelling for long periods without becoming difficult. You know they need a calm, confident rider rather than a tentative one.

Over time, this becomes invisible to you. It feels normal.

A buyer does not inherit your understanding.

If a horse requires experienced handling, a structured routine, turnout with companions, a specific feeding regime, ulcer management, regular bodywork, or consistent exercise to remain settled, that is not a weakness. It is a condition of ownership. Present it as such. The right buyer will respect it. The wrong buyer will step away.

Silence about management rarely protects the horse. It usually transfers risk.

Potential and promise

Potential deserves careful handling.

Foals and yearlings are almost always sold on what they might become. In racing, reining, showing, or performance industries, the horse has not yet proven itself. Value rests on pedigree, conformation, movement, temperament, and early handling. In these cases, potential is not exaggeration. It is the product being offered.

Pedigree carries weight because it suggests probability. Correct conformation supports durability. Good early handling shapes trainability. Buyers of youngstock understand they are purchasing likelihood, not certainty. In some industries, this may be the only stage in a horse's life when it commands a higher price than it ever will again.

Once performance begins, promise is either realised, redirected, or reduced by injury, limited opportunity, or lack of ability.

Even so, potential must be described with restraint. It is reasonable to say that a well-bred foal from proven bloodlines shows promise for a particular discipline. It is not reasonable to imply that success is inevitable. There is a difference between presenting genetic possibility and guaranteeing outcome. Buyers deserve to know the strength of the pedigree, the achievements of close relatives, and any known weaknesses in the line.

A good video here is worth its weight in gold, because the buyer can do their own evaluation without you needing to justify claims of "unlimited" potential.

Selling youngstock ethically means separating evidence from enthusiasm. State what the pedigree has produced. Describe conformation accurately. Be honest about temperament, growth patterns, and handling to date. Potential should rest on observable facts and documented history, not hopeful language.

Breeding stock

Stallions require even greater care.

When you sell a colt or young stallion, you are not only selling his athletic ability. You are selling the possibility of what he may produce. A young stallion with one or two small crops on the ground has not yet proven himself as a sire. What you are presenting is promise, not performance.

Pedigree often carries more influence here than anywhere else. Buyers will study sire lines, dam performance, siblings, and family trends. They will look at conformation not only for how the horse performs, but for what he may pass on. Temperament matters doubly. A talented but difficult stallion may transmit more than ability. If traits run strongly in the family, both strengths and weaknesses should be acknowledged.

Early foals can mislead. One or two outstanding individuals do not establish consistency. Nor does one disappointing foal define a stallion's future. Ethical representation means stating what is known. How many mares has he covered? How many live foals are on the ground? What has been observed so far in type, temperament, and soundness? Avoid suggesting prepotency before it has been demonstrated.

Selling a stallion is selling influence. That influence may shape herds for years. Enthusiasm about a bloodline is understandable, especially if you bred and raised him yourself. But potential as a sire should rest on documented evidence and honest assessment, not marketing language. A stallion's reputation will ultimately be built by the quality and consistency of his progeny, not by early optimism.

Selling broodmares

Broodmares carry a different kind of value. When you sell a mare in foal, empty after a productive career, or with a foal at foot and ready to re-breed, you are not only presenting her as she stands.

You are presenting her reproductive history, her maternal traits, and her genetic contribution.

If a mare is sold in foal, current information matters. A recent veterinary pregnancy diagnosis should be provided, not assumed from last season's scan. Buyers deserve to know the service date, the stallion details, the method of service, and any complications that occurred. If there has been early embryonic loss in the past, that history should be disclosed. In-foal mares are often valued partly on the strength of the covering stallion, but the pregnancy itself is not a guarantee until confirmed and progressing normally.

For empty mares with a strong breeding record, documentation carries weight. Conception rates, ease of foaling, mothering ability, and the quality of progeny all form part of her value. If embryos have been flushed, retained, or sold separately, this should be transparent. Embryo transfer programmes introduce additional variables, and buyers should know what has been done and why. The value of stored embryos, if included in the sale, should be clearly documented and verifiable.

A mare sold with a foal at foot and suitable for re-breeding requires thoughtful presentation. An ethical breeder ensures she is in appropriate body condition, neither run down nor artificially overfed for appearance. The foal should be correctly handled for its age. Vaccination, worming, and breeding dates should be up to date and recorded. If the mare has required assistance at foaling, has had retained membranes, or has shown any reproductive irregularity, this should be stated plainly.

Above all, a broodmare should not be marketed on sentiment alone. "Good mother" must mean more than affection. It should reflect soundness, fertility, temperament, and the ability to raise a foal consistently. Breeding stock represent future responsibility. Presenting a mare honestly protects not only the buyer's investment, but the next generation she may produce.

The quiet omission

There is a difference between deliberate deception and quiet omission. The first is obvious. The second is far more common.

Quiet omission sounds like this:
"It hasn't been an issue recently."
"We haven't seen that for a while."
"He's fine if you ride him regularly."

Each statement may be factually correct. Yet each may conceal a pattern that a buyer cannot see.

If you ever find yourself hoping a buyer does not ask a particular question, pause. That hesitation is information. It signals that something needs to be addressed directly, not skirted around.

You are not protecting the horse by withholding known triggers. You are increasing the chance of conflict later.

Presentation and artificial calm

There are practices that sit firmly on the wrong side of judgement. Sedating a horse before a viewing. Exhausting it beforehand so it appears quieter. Avoiding situations that might reveal genuine behaviour while implying broader suitability.

These are not grey areas. They are decisions.

Even subtler forms of staging deserve attention. Schooling harder than usual before a viewing. Avoiding letting the buyer handle the horse. Controlling every aspect of the assessment so nothing unpredictable occurs.

A horse should be seen as it lives, not as it performs under orchestration.

The phrase “He’s never done that before”

Almost every seller has said it at some point.

Sometimes it is true. Horses surprise us. They react differently in new environments. But if that phrase appears too readily, it becomes a shield.

If you know the horse can react under pressure, say so before the pressure appears. If you know it dislikes certain handling, such as clipping, its ears being touched, or being tied solid, mention it before the buyer discovers it.

Surprises erode trust more quickly than imperfections.

Responsibility beyond convenience

The most difficult grey areas arise when inconvenience collides with principle.

You may need the sale. The market may be slow. The buyer may seem enthusiastic but slightly mismatched. The horse may not be entirely straightforward, yet you believe it will probably be fine.

'Probably' is rarely a steady foundation.

The horse will live with the consequences of your decision long after the cheque clears. So will the buyer.

Ethical selling is not about presenting flawless horses. It is about presenting honestly. It requires tolerating the possibility that a sale may slow down, that the pool of buyers may narrow, or that the price may need reconsideration.

Integrity sometimes costs time. It rarely costs sleep.

The test

When faced with a difficult decision, ask yourself a simple question.

If this detail becomes known later, will I feel at ease explaining it?

If the answer is no, address it now.

Ethical grey areas demand that you describe patterns rather than incidents, that you resist softening language for the sake of convenience, and that you place the long-term welfare of the horse above the speed of the sale.

Most disputes do not arise from malice. They arise from omission, optimism, and discomfort avoided too early. Selling well is not about removing risk. It is about ensuring that risk is shared knowingly.

There will be a suitable buyer for every horse if you do it ethically.

Chapter 12

Setting up the visit

Safety, expectations and assessment

There is a noticeable shift when a buyer moves from talking about a horse to standing next to it. Until that moment, everything has been hypothetical. Once a visit is arranged, the horse becomes physical, and with that comes a different set of responsibilities.

For sellers, this is often where anxiety surfaces. Not because you doubt the horse, but because the variables multiply. New people. New handling. Riding under unfamiliar hands. Questions of safety, liability, and fairness move from abstract to immediate.

Once a buyer decides to visit, move from conversation to logistics. Set a specific, agreed time. Avoid vague or open-ended arrangements. A clear appointment respects everyone involved and reduces the risk of rushed arrivals, missed expectations, or disruption to the horse's routine.

Provide clear directions and contact details in advance. Do not assume navigation apps will suffice, particularly in rural areas. Simple written directions and any relevant gate or access instructions help buyers arrive calm rather than flustered. Find out how far they will be coming.

Before the visit takes place, be clear about what will and will not happen. Who will ride the horse? Under what circumstances? With which equipment? Explain what riding gear is required, whether the buyer should bring their own saddle and whether helmets and boots are non-negotiable. Clarify whether whether photos or video may be taken and if dogs are welcome or should remain in the car. What about children? If there are non-negotiables, state them early rather than managing them on the day.

Some buyers arrive with strong emotion. They may speak of lifelong dreams or forever homes early. This is understandable, but it should not override your (or their) judgement.

Others will arrive with horse float and cash in their pocket. Some may begin negotiating price before suitability has been properly assessed, or offer to pay in advance of the scheduled viewing. None of this obliges you to move faster than you are comfortable with.

Buyers sometimes assume arrangements will be negotiable once they arrive. When expectations are left unspoken, sellers can find themselves agreeing to situations they would not have accepted calmly beforehand. (How do you think I know this?)

Clear communication ahead of time prevents this.

Decide where you will greet the buyer. This might be your kitchen with coffee already on, a small office with records, trophies and photos, or a tidy stable or arena area where the horse can be caught and viewed easily. Let buyers know where toilet facilities are. Small details allow focus to stay on the horse.

When the buyer arrives, introduce yourself with a handshake and a moment of acknowledgement. This establishes a calm, professional tone from the outset.

An office or trophy area makes a nice meeting place.

Safety, responsibility, and boundaries

A visit should never be improvised. By the time the buyer arrives, you should already have considered safety, responsibility, and how the horse will be presented. This includes ensuring your public liability insurance is current and taking reasonable steps to minimise risk.

It is entirely reasonable to explain that you, or the horse's regular rider, will demonstrate the horse first. It is reasonable to limit riding to certain gaits, exercises, or environments, such as a round yard. Saying no to jumping, fast work, or unfamiliar situations is appropriate if those activities are not part of the horse's usual routine.

Equipment and risk management

Equipment is not a minor detail. You are entitled to insist on correct, well-fitting gear, including appropriate helmets, boots, and safety equipment. If a buyer intends to ride, it is reasonable to ask them to bring their own saddle where appropriate, or to limit riding to tack you know fits the horse well.

Poorly fitting saddles or unfamiliar equipment introduce unnecessary variables. They affect comfort, behaviour, and interpretation, and they increase risk. It is reasonable to place a child or anxious rider on a lead rein or the lunge to begin with and to give basic instructions.

If something feels wrong, you are probably correct. *You are not obliged to proceed.*

Allow enough time

Allow enough time for the horse to be seen properly and for the questions that naturally follow. Buyers need space to observe, think, and ask without feeling hurried toward a decision.

By all means, ask the buyer how much time they have. If they have a deadline, they will let you know. This allows you to pace yourself, show photos and records, and perhaps other related horses. This is particularly valuable if you are selling a foal or broodmare.

In most situations, allowing up to two hours is reasonable. Most visits will not use more than an hour, but knowing it is available changes the tone. Buyers relax. Conversations become clearer. Decisions are more considered.

Trying to fit a visit into a narrow window can create unnecessary tension. Horses feel it. Buyers feel it. Important details are more easily missed.

Evaluating the horse on the ground

Always begin on the ground before anyone gets on. This may include catching the horse, leading it in, tying up, picking up feet, and allowing the buyer to walk around it quietly. Walking and trotting the horse up on a straight line provides useful information about movement, soundness, and manners.

Buyers may feel suspicious if, when they arrive, the horse is already saddled for them to mount. I have had this happen to me more than once; one horse turned out to be difficult to catch, another had been worked down before my visit to make it appear much quieter than it really was.

An inexperienced buyer may not think to ask. Doing it anyway provides guidance and transparency that sets a calm, methodical tone.

Allow simple interaction so you can assess confidence and competence.

Stroking, brushing, or leading allows buyers to observe temperament and character without pressure. This is particularly useful with a young horse that can be led over or around obstacles, walk onto a float or truck, be rugged or un-rugged, and be taken away from its mates. Each of these offers useful information.

Evaluating the horse under saddle

It is important for your horse's regular rider to demonstrate first. This shows the horse going as it normally does and provides context. If a warm-up is required, this can be explained at the same time.

Begin in an enclosed area with simple work. Avoid long or demanding sessions. When the buyer rides, pay attention to anything that feels uncharacteristic or concerning, including:

- signs of discomfort with a new rider
- unusual tension, tail swishing, head shaking, or rushing
- insensitive riding or blocking the horse's normal movement
- requests for work the horse is not prepared for
- pressure to ride off property, with or without supervision

How to stop

You should feel comfortable stepping in. Ending a ride early is sometimes the most responsible decision. You might say:

- I think we should leave it there for now.
- I don't believe this is the right match.
- I'm going to call it here.
- I'm not happy to continue.
- I don't feel good about how this is lining up.
- I think stopping now is the sensible option.

- I would rather be cautious than have someone get hurt.

Notice something important? None of these criticise the rider. None accuse. None debate skill. They are decisions, not arguments. You do not need lengthy explanations. Stating that you do not believe the horse is the right fit is sufficient. Continuing once that conclusion is reached helps no one.

A professional boundary is much easier to defend later than a reluctant 'yes'. Sure, there will be disappointment, but deep down, the buyer knows this to be true.

If pressure appears before or during a visit, pause and ask yourself:

- Has this horse been assessed properly yet?
- Is the buyer focused on match or outcome?
- Am I being asked to skip steps I consider important?
- Would I make the same decision if there were no urgency?

Before the visit ends

Ask if they have seen everything they wish to see. Check where the buyer is at in their thinking. Keen interest may be shown by questions about transport, transfers, and future management. If they are unsure, ask what they are unsure about. Invite clarity without demanding a decision.

Some buyers appreciate time to think or to speak privately with a coach or family member. You may ask if they would like to speak to their support person privately in their car, while you put the horse away. Others take video to show to their coach. Ask how long they need to consider their options and *be clear about how long you are prepared to hold the horse.*

Twenty-four hours is reasonable, or until a vet check outcome if discussed.

Off-property assessment

Some buyers ask to see a horse at a neutral venue. It is quite normal for a buyer to ask to see a competition horse in a competitive environment. You are not obliged to agree to off-property trials however. Do so only if it genuinely serves the assessment. This can be useful but introduces additional considerations. If you agree, expectations must be explicit:

- who transports the horse
- who rides first
- what will be asked of the horse

- who is responsible if something goes wrong

When buyers do not turn up

Missed appointments are frustrating and costly, and they happen more often than sellers expect. By the time a visit is arranged, time has already been invested in preparation, scheduling, and the horse's routine.

If a buyer fails to attend without notice:

- follow up once, politely
- avoid rescheduling unless there was a genuine misunderstanding
- continue with other enquiries

Treat this as information rather than an insult. A buyer who does not respect your time at this stage rarely becomes easier to deal with later.

If the buyer wishes to proceed

Sometimes a buyer will proceed subject to further conditions such as a second ride or a vet check. Unless you have several buyers in line, I suggest you agree to this.

If instead, it is subject to them being able to organize their finances, you dropping the price so they can afford it, or having to get hubby to agree to them purchasing a horse, these are things they needed to *sort out before looking at the horse*! It is not up to you to provide credit or payment plans or anything else likely to hold up a clean sale, unless you have spoken about this previously.

This is the time to discuss practicalities if the sale goes ahead: collection date, agistment (if delayed) and how this will be documented, whether the horse needs a float-loading reminder or vaccinations, before travel.

If a horse remains on your property, clarify the rate, what is included, payment timing (I suggest at least two weeks in advance), responsibility for veterinary care, insurance, and emergency decisions.

Different horses carry different paperwork. Registration certificates, breed society transfers, performance records, membership numbers, passports, and microchip details do not always move automatically or instantly. Explain what will transfer, what requires forms or fees, and roughly when this will occur.

When is a horse actually sold?

A horse is not sold until the money is in your bank account. Not promised. Not screenshot. Not pending. Not when someone says they are "waiting on the bank."

Once payment is made, responsibility changes to the buyer, even if the horse has not yet left. Before the buyer leaves, clarify:

- what documents exist
- which documents will transfer
- when transfer will occur
- who is responsible for fees
- who lodges paperwork (should be within 30 days)
- what proof of transfer the buyer can expect

This reassures serious buyers and signals professionalism. A well-prepared visit does not guarantee a sale, but it does guarantee something more important. The horse has been represented honestly, the buyer has been given space to assess suitability, and no one has been rushed into a decision they may later regret.

A well-run visit does not close a sale. It opens the right one.

When more than one buyer is interested

Sometimes interest overlaps. You may have a viewing booked while another buyer wants to move quickly. Someone may offer to pay in full before others have seen the horse. A buyer travelling from a distance may ask you to hold the horse until they arrive.

There is no single correct response. What matters is that you are clear, consistent, and transparent. You do not owe everyone the same outcome. You do owe everyone the same honesty.

- If a viewing is scheduled, it is reasonable to say so.
- If the horse is not being held, say that clearly.
- If you intend to decide only after a visit, state it upfront.

Incident record and subsequent claim

About 25 years ago, we had an incident which resulted in a claim against us

What occurred on the day

A buyer attended the property to inspect and trial the horse after prior discussions in which the horse had been advertised as green broken, with approximately four weeks of work and needing further education. She assured us her last horse was a 'rogue Arabian', which she'd re-trained. She offered to pay a holding deposit, which we declined.

She travelled to us from Ballarat (about 8 hours) though warned it would be a very hot day (38C). She arrived wearing heavy clothes and a jumper, and appeared to be considerably overweight.

Upon arrival she walked up the hill with my teenage daughter to view the horses in the paddock so she could see their general temperament and how they interacted with people. The horse, a two year old gelding was then brought in.

The horse was first demonstrated on the lunge so she could see what he had been taught. During this time she stated she had *not ridden for five years*! She was told she should ride in the yard but refused because there wasn't enough room to canter.

The ridden demonstration took place further up the hill, with my daughter riding. Under her the horse behaved quietly, consistent with a young, newly started horse. When the demonstration finished the visitor put on her helmet and indicated she wished to ride.

The stirrups were adjusted. She had difficulty reaching the iron and commented that her clothing was not stretchy. A log was offered as a mounting aid and she agreed to use it.

During repeated attempts the horse shifted position in small movements, which is common while mounting, especially with a heavy rider. Though she had indicated she was experienced, she had to be reminded to take up the reins.

By this time she had mounted part way. The horse moved away, first in trot and then in a couple of canter strides. She was not seated in the saddle and fell to the off side.

Assistance was given immediately. She said her ankle hurt. She briefly mentioned dizziness and that she might have hit her head, then continued to focus on the ankle. She sat, then later stood and walked.

At her request her car was brought closer. Ice and water were provided at the house. Conversation remained friendly. She indicated she might instead look for an older, quieter horse (her friend's previous suggestion).

My daughter suggested it might not be a good idea to drive home. She said she might stay at a friends house at Murray Bridge, only an hour away. At the time of departure there was no suggestion of hostility. And as it turned out she drove all the way home.

To our surprise, a claim was received three days later.

In the correspondence, she attested that the incident had occurred because of alleged shortcomings in how the horse had been represented and managed during the trial.

Among the matters she raised were assertions, as we understood them, that:

- the horse behaved in a way she later characterised as bolting or playing up
- she should not have been allowed to mount
- different or additional precautions should have been taken
- she had suffered injury as a consequence
- it was inappropriate for a young person to demonstrate the horse

Our position regarding those assertions

We maintained that the horse had been consistently described, in advertising and conversation, as green broken, newly started, and requiring further education.

- We had discussed that young horses have an unpredictable element and require continued exposure to new experiences.
- She did not state before arrival that she had lost confidence or considered herself unable to ride such a horse.
- On the day she was offered alternatives, including riding in the yard or not riding. She chose to proceed.
- The movements of the horse during mounting were minor and typical. The horse did not run off uncontrollably, it moved forward while she was insecurely positioned.
- Immediate assistance was provided. She was mobile, declined medical attendance, accepted ice and water, and left on amicable terms.

Additional contextual factors noted

- The day was extremely hot, as reported elsewhere.
- She had walked up and down the hill and remained dressed in heavier clothing, despite having brought more suitable attire.
- She had travelled a long distance that day and intended to return the same day.
- She stated we should not have given responsibility for the sale to a teenager. However, my daughter broke the horse in, and at the time was employed as a professional horse-breaker for the SA Mounted Police.

Outcome

The matter was referred promptly to our insurer. After review, the insurer advised there was no case to answer. The claim was subsequently withdrawn.

Key learnings

Red flags that should stop a ride

- Vague, inconsistent, or changing accounts of riding experience
- Long periods out of the saddle, especially when looking at a young or newly started horse
- Emotional commitment to buying before the horse is even tried, urgency, pressure to mount, or worry someone else will buy first
- Difficulty explaining how they cope with normal issues like shying, speed, or loss of balance
- Describing previous horses as entirely at fault
- Turning up tired, overheated, or under-prepared, such as unsuitable clothing or footwear for safe mounting and riding

Chapter 13

Vet checks

and the involvement of third parties

As buyers become more serious, it is common for another voice to enter the process. A trusted friend. A mentor. A coach. Sometimes a professional who will not ultimately be riding the horse, but whose opinion carries weight. This is normal.

Trainers, coaches, and advisers

Experienced buyers rarely make decisions alone. Third-party input is usually about self-protection, not mistrust. Your role does not change when professionals are involved.

You should not attempt to convince, justify, debate, criticize or override professional advice. Sellers who remain calm at this stage often find that trust deepens rather than erodes.

The vet check

A vet check should not be treated like a hurdle to clear but rather a process to understand. For sellers, it can feel exposing. For buyers, it can feel decisive. In reality, it is neither a verdict nor a negotiation tool. It is information.

Handled well, a vet check protects everyone involved. Handled poorly, it creates pressure, misunderstanding, and lingering resentment long after the sale should have settled.

Make sure your horse will allow picking up of legs, have its teeth examined, and stand calmly for routine examination. It will also need to be trotted out, and possibly lunged and ridden. It may involve you travelling the horse to a clinic for specialised evaluation.

Make sure your buyer is using an experienced equine vet.

So often a sale falls through because the nearest vet is used, rather than an experienced equine vet. Also make sure you are present at the check. Don't leave it up to the trainer or someone else involved with the horse.

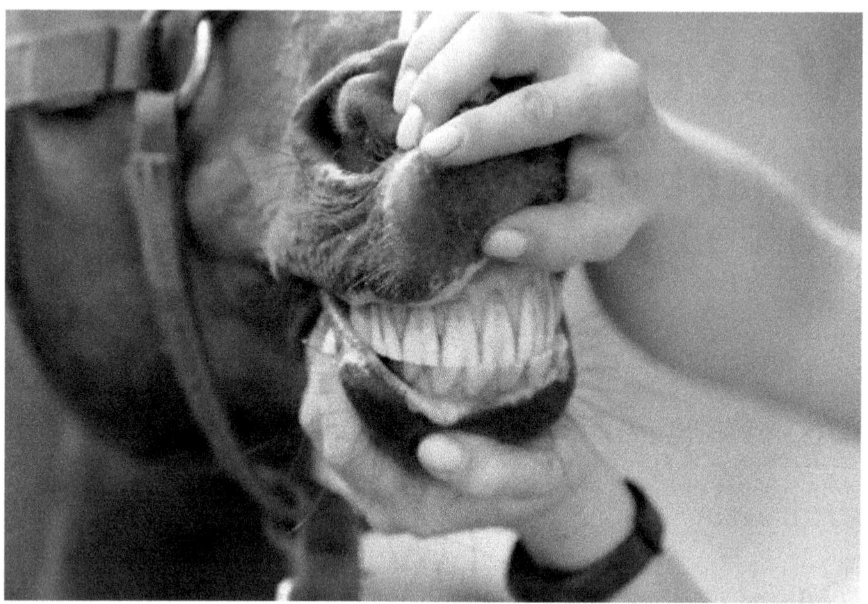

Make sure your horse is familiar with having its teeth examined.

What buyers are really seeking

Predictability and suitability, rather than perfection, is what a buyer is looking for. A vet check is about understanding risk in relation to intended use. A finding that is irrelevant for one buyer may be decisive for another. This is why vet check results do not exist in isolation. Sellers who understand this remain steady when third parties enter the process.

Your role is not to interpret findings for the buyer or influence the outcome. Your role is to allow the process to occur cleanly and without interference. This includes:

- allowing the buyer to use their chosen veterinarian
- providing access to the horse and its history as agreed
- answering factual questions, while avoiding minimisation, or omission

It is reasonable to clarify what level of exam is being requested and how results will be handled. It is not appropriate to question conclusions. But you can ask for a second opinion.

Scope and expectations

Not every vet check is the same. Some buyers request a basic clinical exam. Others require imaging. Some are guided by insurance requirements rather than concern. This avoids surprise and helps frame the outcome realistically. Before the examination, it is reasonable to clarify:

- the scope of the vet check
- whether imaging is expected
- whether bloods will be taken
- whether findings will be shared with you
- blood tests and medication declarations

Blood testing is now standard practice in many sales, particularly where competition, insurance, or higher value is involved.

As the seller, you should expect:

- bloods to be taken and retained by the veterinarian
- a declaration to be signed by you outlining any treatments, medications, or supplements given within a defined period (commonly the previous 7 days)
- confirmation that the horse has not been medicated with prohibited substances unless under veterinary supervision and disclosed

It is sensible to request that blood samples be **retained for a minimum of seven days after the horse has been collected**, or longer if advised. This protects both of you if questions arise later about sedation, pain relief, or prohibited substances.

Communication between veterinarians

In some cases, the buyer's veterinarian may wish to speak directly with your veterinarian, particularly if:

- the horse has a known veterinary history
- imaging or previous reports exist
- the buyer is purchasing from a distance

This is normal. It is reasonable to facilitate factual exchange while remaining clear that professional opinions are not yours to manage or reconcile. You may also request copies of:

- written reports
- imaging summaries
- declarations or disclosures provided to the buyer's vet

This ensures that information shared about the horse is accurate and consistent, and avoids confusion later.

When a horse 'fails' a vet check

A horse does not fail a vet check. A buyer decides not to proceed based on the information received. This distinction matters.

A finding that ends one sale does not define the horse. It may relate to future risk, insurance exclusions, or the buyer's personal tolerance rather than current soundness. If a vet check results in withdrawal:

- ask for a written summary
- understand what the concern actually is
- clarify whether it is current, historical, or speculative
- resist emotional reactions

Many sales unravel here not because of the finding, but because of how it is handled.

Disclosure after a 'failed' vet check

If a horse has previously failed a vet check on a material issue, that information should not be concealed.

However, disclosure works best with timing and context. Dropping veterinary history into early messages without explanation may creates alarm. Later in the process, a calm explanation, what was found, when, and why it mattered, allows a buyer to assess its relevance rather than react to labels.

Conflicting opinions

It is common for professionals to disagree. One vet may be comfortable with a finding. Another may not. One trainer may see potential. Another may see limitation. This reflects differences in risk tolerance, not right or wrong. Allow the buyer to weigh the advice they have sought.

You are entitled to suggest another opinion.

When a sale pauses or ends

If a buyer walks away after a vet check, it is rarely personal. Information changes decisions. That is the point of gathering it.

A sale that ends here has not failed. It has done what it needed to do.

If circumstances change mid-process

If a horse becomes sick or injured during the selling process, the sale must pause. A buyer should be informed promptly and honestly. Continuing as if nothing has changed undermines trust and exposes you to unnecessary risk.

In many cases, the correct response is to withdraw the horse temporarily until it can be assessed fairly again. That is professionalism.

Responsibility during the vetting phase

Until payment has cleared and ownership has transferred, responsibility remains with the seller. This includes:

- veterinary care
- management decisions
- suitability for sale

Buyers should not be asked to absorb risk for a horse they do not yet own.

Optional checklist

After a vet check, confirm you have:

□ a copy of the full vetting report

□ any imaging or blood test results provided to the buyer

□ clarity on what advice was given verbally

□ confirmation of whether the buyer's vet spoke to your vet

□ a shared understanding of any findings or limitations

□ if another opinion has been sought

Lame foal

Many years ago, we sold a foal, subject to final payment at weaning. During this time it became lame. Understandably, we advised the buyer who immediately ordered a vet check. Her vet concluded after doing nerve blocks, but without x-rays, that the foal had "genetic ringbone."

We thought this was rather odd, as there was no familial history for it to be genetic, and rather young to have developed ringbone. We wondered how he could make this conclusion without xrays. The buyer immediately cancelled that sale, forfeiting her deposit, even though I suggested getting xrays, or another opinion.

A few days later, an abcess burst out, and the foal was no longer sore. We rang the lady to tell her and that she could get the foal re-examined. Her answer was "I have been advised never to buy a lame horse. Good-day." We sold the horse later to a person who enjoyed a long life with him.

When one door closes, another one always opens.

Package

We once sold five horses to Mr X, over 1000ks away. He was one of the richest landowners in Australia, and he wanted to start a breeding programme of Australian Stock Horses on his multiple outback station properties. His representative chose them, and we subsequently awaited confirmation.

A very short time later, we received a phone call from a transport company advising us that they would be picking up the horses the next day. I informed them the horses would be going nowhere as payment had not been made.

Within ten minutes I received a call from the representative to state that they would be providing payment upon receiving a 30 day invoice, as that is how Mr X's business empire "operated".

"Don't worry" she said, "you will get paid." My reply to her was that if they wanted the horses to be collected tomorrow, they would need to provide payment today, as that was how '*we operated*.'

The money was dropped into our account that day.

Chapter 14

Conditions that hold together

Without regret

Up until now, much of the process has been conversational. Interest has been expressed. A visit may have taken place. Everyone may feel they are on the same page.

This is where sellers sometimes relax too early, assuming goodwill will carry the sale through. This is the point where a sale either settles cleanly into place, or begins to drift. Anything you put in writing before a sale is completed may be used later if there is a dispute.

Messages, emails, advertisements, and written answers to questions can all be treated as evidence of what was represented or implied at the time of sale. This is not a reason to be guarded or evasive, but it is a reason to be deliberate.

For this reason, most well-constructed contracts include a clause stating that the written agreement replaces and overrides any prior discussions, representations, or understandings.

In plain terms, this means:

- the contract records what has been agreed
- earlier conversations do not continue to operate alongside it
- expectations are anchored to one shared document

This ensures that responsibility is defined deliberately, not pieced together later from memory, messages, or goodwill.

If something matters enough to rely on, it should appear in the contract.

Contracts, deposits, and conditions

Contracts should record what was agreed, not attempt to guarantee outcomes beyond your control. Most disputes arise not from dishonesty, but from absolute language applied to variable realities.

Avoid absolute statements in contracts or written correspondence about soundness, suitability, or future performance. Horses change. Context matters. Guarantees invite problems where none were intended.

A note for high-value and competition sales

Where a horse is higher value, highly trained, or competing at an established level, expectations shift on both sides.

Buyers are often experienced, decisive, and operating within tight schedules. They may be purchasing from a distance, relying on video, professional opinion, and veterinary information rather than repeated visits. Travel, insurance, and timing carry greater weight.

In these sales, it is reasonable to expect:

- earlier discussion of vetting scope and preferred veterinarians
- clear agreement on when risk transfers, particularly if transport is delayed
- explicit handling of insurance from the moment funds clear
- firm timelines around payment, collection, and documentation

It is also common for buyers to request:

- full competition footage rather than highlights
- professional references or performance records
- a defined decision window rather than open-ended negotiation

Red flags worth pausing for

Most sales proceed smoothly. When they do not, warning signs are usually present early and easy to rationalise away.

No single item below means a sale should not proceed. What matters is pattern, pressure, and timing.

Signals that deserve a pause

- The buyer pushes to move quickly while avoiding practical questions
- Payment is offered immediately, but collection, paperwork, or management remains vague
- Screenshots of "pending" transfers replace cleared funds
- Stories about forever homes appear early and substitute for concrete plans
- Resistance to written terms or defensiveness when details are clarified
- Small details shift repeatedly (dates, names, arrangements)
- You feel rushed into accepting something you would normally consider carefully

Free or reduced-price placements

When a horse is given away, or placed well below market value, structure becomes more important, not less. Good intentions do not protect horses.

A "free horse" is still a transfer of ownership, responsibility, and risk. If those elements are left vague, misunderstandings arise quickly, particularly if the placement later breaks down.

Common conditions sellers may reasonably attach include:

Return conditions
You may require that the horse be returned to you if the placement does not work, rather than sold on or passed to a third party. If this is important, it must be stated clearly:

- whether return is mandatory or optional
- under what circumstances return applies
- who pays for transport
- whether there is a time limit on the return condition

Without this in writing, the new owner is usually free to rehome or sell the horse as they choose.

No resale or right-of-first-refusal clauses

Some sellers wish to prevent a horse being sold on, or want the first option to buy the horse back if it is ever rehomed. These conditions should specify:

- whether resale is prohibited or conditional
- whether you must be notified before any transfer
- whether a price cap or buy-back amount applies

Ambiguity here is one of the most common sources of conflict in free placements.

Intended use and care expectations

You may wish to specify how the horse is intended to be used (for example, companion only, light riding, no breeding, no competition).

If these expectations matter to you, they should be written plainly, without judgement or emotion.

Ownership and transfer date

Even when no money changes hands, the agreement should state:

- the date ownership transfers
- when responsibility and risk transfer
- whether insurance is expected or required

A free horse without a transfer date is still legally owned by someone. Uncertainty here benefits no one. Without a legal agreement, the new carer could charge say, veterinary expenses to you, claiming the horse was yours. Free placements often feel informal because money is not involved. When expectations are written down calmly and clearly, they protect the horse from instability and protect both parties from resentment later.

Documentation

Any registration papers, passports, or identification documents should be accounted for:

- whether they transfer to the new owner
- when the transfer will occur
- who lodges the paperwork

If papers are retained deliberately (for example, to prevent breeding or resale), that should be stated explicitly.

A horse placed thoughtfully, even without a price tag, deserves the same care in agreement as one sold at full value.

Deposits: what they actually do

A deposit is not a guarantee that a sale will proceed. It holds space while specific conditions are met. Ten to twenty percent of the purchase price is commonly considered reasonable. Before accepting a deposit, three questions should already be answered:

- What does the deposit secure?
- For how long?
- Under what circumstances, if any, is it refundable?

There is no universally correct approach. There is only the approach you can explain, apply consistently, and stand behind.

Payment promised but not received

A horse is not sold until the money has cleared into your account. Screenshots, pending transactions, or verbal assurances are not payment. Scammers rely on urgency and trust. Calm verification protects you. Until funds are received:

- the horse remains available
- ownership does not transfer
- no arrangements should be finalised

Cooling-off periods (jurisdiction dependent)

In some jurisdictions, contracts may be subject to a statutory cooling-off period. In others, they are not. This can depend on where you live, whether the sale is private or conducted through a business, and how the agreement is structured.

Sellers should not assume that a cooling-off period applies, nor assume that it does not.

Where a cooling-off period exists, it may allow a buyer to withdraw within a defined timeframe, sometimes subject to conditions, costs, or exclusions. In horse sales, these rights are often limited, particularly once the horse has been ridden, vetted, transported, or used in any way.

Because this varies widely, it is important to:

- understand whether a cooling-off period applies in your state or country
- know whether it applies to private sales, dealer sales, or both
- clarify whether it can be waived by agreement

- state clearly in the contract what applies in your case

Uncertainty around cooling-off rights is a common source of misunderstanding after a sale. Addressing this early prevents assumptions from filling the gaps.

If you are unsure, seek local legal advice before the contract is signed. It is far easier to clarify this upfront than to untangle it later.

Returns, trials, and assumptions

In private sales, return rights do not exist by default. Unless a right of return is created deliberately and in writing, the sale is final once payment has cleared and ownership has transferred. Silence does not create flexibility. It creates uncertainty.

If a trial, return window, or conditional sale is offered, it must define:

- duration
- location
- responsibility for risk (e.g. injury) and costs
- grounds for return
- responsibility and time frame for return

Delayed collection and responsibility

If a horse is not collected immediately, the agreed date and consequences of delay must be stated clearly. Sellers often assume prompt collection. Buyers often assume flexibility. Delays without communication should not be absorbed silently. Follow up with a simple written instruction to prevent confusion. When collection is delayed:

- clarify whether agistment applies
- state the rate and inclusions
- confirm who carries responsibility and risk
- set a revised collection deadline

Buyer remorse

Buyer remorse is common, particularly after emotionally loaded decisions. It does not automatically mean the sale was wrong.

If the horse was represented honestly and the agreement was clear, remorse is something the buyer will need to work through. Be cautious of emotional pressure dressed up as consequence, for example threats of immediate resale or damage to your reputation. Reopening sound agreements simply to relieve discomfort rarely ends well.

However, if you believe you have misjudged the kind of home the horse has gone to, then the decision becomes personal. It is up to you whether you want to take the horse back, and if you do, under what conditions.

Common contract structures (plain English)

Different situations call for different agreements. None are inherently wrong. Each carries consequences that should be understood in everyday terms.

Outright sale (clean transfer)

Buyer pulls notes from his pocket. Responsibility shifts to the new owner. The horse is collected. Paperwork transfers. This is the simplest arrangement and the least prone to dispute.

In an outright sale, you should provide either a receipt, a tax invoice, or a Bill of Sale. These documents serve different purposes, but all confirm that a transaction has taken place.

A receipt or tax invoice confirms that payment has been made. At a minimum, it should include:

- the date of sale
- the names and contact details of buyer and seller
- a clear description of the horse
- the amount paid
- confirmation that payment has been received in full

If you are selling as a *business*, a tax invoice may also need to include business details and any applicable tax information, depending on your jurisdiction.

A Bill of Sale goes a step further. It records not just payment, but transfer of ownership. It typically states:

- the identity of the horse
- the agreed purchase price
- the date ownership transfers

- the names and contact details of buyer and seller
- that the horse is sold outright, without conditions unless stated

A Bill of Sale does not guarantee soundness, suitability, or future performance. It records the moment responsibility changes hands.

For most private sales, either a receipt or a simple Bill of Sale is sufficient. What matters is that the document reflects what actually occurred: payment cleared, ownership transferred, and no conditions remain outstanding. Clear paperwork closes the sale.

Deposit with conditions

The horse is held while agreed conditions are met. Risk lies not in the deposit, but in vague terms around refunds and timelines.

Payment plans

Payment over time blurs responsibility unless handled carefully. Ownership, insurance, and default consequences must be explicit. In most private sales, these arrangements carry more risk than they appear to.

Agistment after sale

If ownership has transferred, but the horse remains in the seller's care, this becomes a service arrangement, not an extension of the sale. Rates and decision-making must be clear. These conditions can be arranged separately, *or* included in the sales contract.

Broodmare, embryo, foal and reproductive contracts

Everyday questions matter more than legal language. These agreements must address payment, timing, expected care, handling, and veterinary work, delivery and transfer dates, and what happens if circumstances change such as:

- What happens if the mare fails to conceive?
- If an embryo is lost, who bears the cost?
- If a surrogate mare becomes ill or dies, what happens next?
- When does ownership of the resulting foal transfer?

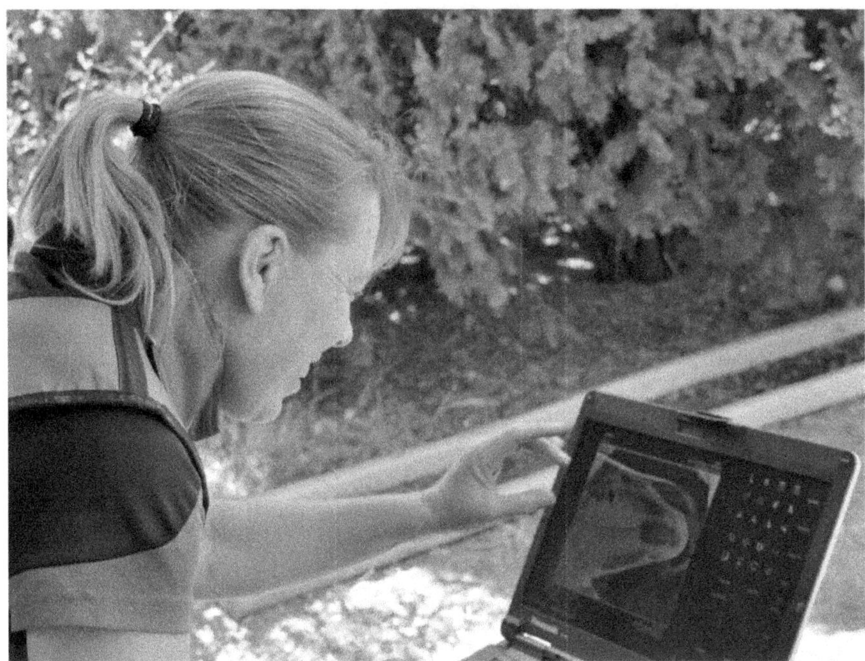

A breeding exam is usually required for insurance and broodmare sales

Stallion sales: additional matters

Selling a stallion carries obligations that do not exist with geldings or mares. Much of a stallion's value sits not only in the horse himself, but in registrations, reproductive material, and existing breeding commitments. These do not automatically transfer with ownership unless they are addressed deliberately.

Before a stallion sale proceeds, the following should be stated clearly: what exists, what transfers, what does not, and who remains responsible for anything outstanding.

Registration and sire status

Confirm the stallion's current registration status and eligibility to breed within the relevant studbook or breed associations. Clarify:

- whether the stallion is fully registered and approved as a sire
- whether DNA typing has been completed and recorded
- whether any additional mandatory testing, such as for genetic diseases or inspection is still required
- who is responsible for completing and paying for any outstanding steps

Do not assume the buyer can "finish this later" without cost or consequence. If registration or approval is incomplete, that affects value and future use.

Semen collection and ownership

If semen has been collected, frozen, or stored, ownership must be defined. Clarify:

- whether semen exists and where it is stored
- who legally owns the semen at the time of sale
- whether ownership of existing semen transfers with the stallion or remains with the seller
- if the new stallion owner has right of first option on sale of semen
- whether storage contracts exist and who is responsible for ongoing fees
- who is authorised to sign release or transfer paperwork

Semen does not automatically follow the stallion. Silence here allows disputes.

Breeding rights and outstanding commitments

Establish whether any breeding obligations exist that were entered into before the sale. Good faith is not a substitute for written understandings. These may include:

- live foal guarantees
- free returns or repeat breedings
- prepaid services
- signed breeding certificates not yet issued

Clarify:

- whether these commitments transfer to the new owner or remain the seller's responsibility
- whether the buyer is expected to honour any prior guarantees
- whether any commitments become void upon change of ownership
- if something will not transfer, say so explicitly.
- responsibility if death of one of the parties for signing records, semen sales and the like.

Documentation still outstanding

Identify any paperwork that exists but has not yet been completed. This may include:

- breeding certificates
- service records
- DNA submissions
- registry transfers
- stallion approval documentation

State clearly:

- what has already been completed
- what remains outstanding
- who will complete it
- who will pay the associated fees

What becomes null and void upon sale

Some rights, guarantees, or arrangements are personal to the seller and do not survive a change of ownership. If these are not separated, disputes tend to arise years later, not immediately. When in doubt, list everything and allocate responsibility plainly. This can include:

- informal breeding promises
- verbal guarantees
- discounted services
- prior understandings not documented

The contract should state that:

- only written terms survive the sale
- any prior arrangements not expressly included are void

This protects both parties from assumptions made by third parties after ownership changes.

A practical reminder

Stallion sales are rarely simple because the horse is rarely the only asset involved. A clear agreement should distinguish between:

- the horse
- genetic material
- paperwork
- promises already made

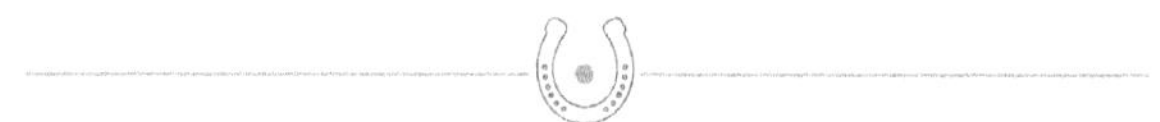

Insurance

Including an insurance clause covering death or injury before final conditions are met is not unreasonable. You might provide a shortlist of respected insurers relevant to the class of horse being sold. This can be a practical guide for buyers.

Insurance clauses: what should be covered

Insurance clauses are not about mistrust. They exist because horses are valuable, unpredictable, and vulnerable to change, particularly during transition periods.

At a minimum, any contract that extends beyond a simple 'payment clears, horse leaves' sale should clarify **who insures the horse, from when, and for what**.

The basics to address are straightforward.

When insurance responsibility transfers

State clearly the moment at which the buyer becomes responsible for insuring the horse. In most cases, this is:

- when funds clear, not when the horse is collected
- If ownership has transferred but the horse remains on the seller's property, this needs to be explicit.

What risks are covered, and by whom

Clarify who bears the risk if the horse:

- becomes ill or injured
- suffers accidental injury or death

- requires emergency veterinary treatment
- damages property

This matters most when there is:

- delayed collection
- a deposit held with conditions
- transport pending
- a vet check or trial window still open

Insurance during delayed collection or agistment

If the horse remains with the seller after the sale is agreed:

- state whether the buyer is expected to insure immediately
- clarify whether the seller's insurance ceases or remains secondary
- confirm who authorises and pays for emergency treatment

Agistment is a service, not an extension of ownership. Insurance responsibility should reflect that.

Mortality and major medical (where relevant)

For higher-value, breeding, or competition horses, buyers may insure for:

- mortality
- major medical
- loss of use

You do not need to mandate this, but it is reasonable to:

- ask whether insurance is in place
- specify that uninsured loss after ownership transfers sits with the buyer

Transport risk

Transport is one of the highest-risk moments in a sale process, and assumptions here are common. If the horse is being transported by a professional company, they will generally have their own insurance. Nonetheless with all travel:

- clarify whether insurance is expected to be active before loading

- confirm who bears risk during transit

If insurance is not in place

If the buyer chooses not to insure, this should be acknowledged. Silence can imply shared responsibility when none was intended.

A simple statement that the buyer assumes all risk from the point of ownership transfer is often sufficient.

Insuring your horse, requires full ID, and Declaration of Health or Vet Check.

If the horse is already insured by the seller

Insurance policies are held by people, not horses. A policy taken out by the seller does not automatically transfer with ownership, even if the horse remains on the same property for a short period. Where a seller already has insurance in place, one of the following must be agreed and recorded:

Option 1: The seller's insurance ceases at ownership transfer
This is the most common and cleanest arrangement.

Once funds clear and ownership transfers, the seller's policy ends or no longer applies to the horse. From that moment, the buyer is responsible for arranging insurance, regardless of when the horse is collected.

This should be stated explicitly, particularly if collection is delayed.

Option 2: The seller's insurance remains temporarily in place (by agreement)
In some situations, the seller may agree to maintain insurance for a defined, short period after the sale. This is most common where:

- collection is delayed by transport logistics
- the buyer is arranging insurance and needs a brief overlap
- the horse is remaining on the seller's property under an agistment arrangement

If this occurs, it must be clear:

- how long the seller's insurance remains in place
- what risks it covers
- whether the buyer contributes to the premium
- that this is temporary and does not imply retained ownership

Without this clarity, insurance can be assumed where none exists.

Option 3: Insurance continues only until the horse leaves the property
Some sellers prefer to maintain insurance until the horse physically departs, even if ownership has already transferred. If this approach is taken, the contract should still state:

- that ownership and responsibility have transferred
- that insurance coverage is limited to the horse remaining on the property
- that transport risk sits with the buyer unless otherwise agreed

This avoids confusion if an incident occurs during loading or transit.

Warning

Never assume an existing policy "covers everyone" during transition. Always check with your insurer at this time. This protects both parties and prevents disputes at the exact moment responsibility changes. If a claim arises, insurers will look closely at:

- who owned the horse at the time of loss
- who held the policy
- what the contract stated about risk and responsibility

If the horse is insured at the time of sale, the contract should state plainly:

- whether that insurance continues
- for how long
- and when the buyer's responsibility begins

A practical note for sellers

While you should not provide insurance advice, it is sensible to:

- know which insurers commonly cover the type of horse you are selling
- suggest that buyers arrange cover before funds clear

This is particularly helpful in competition, breeding, or interstate sales.

Legal advice and templates

This chapter is not legal advice, nor is it intended to replace it. Horse sales sit at the intersection of property law, consumer law, and animal welfare, and requirements vary widely by jurisdiction.

If the sale involves higher value, breeding rights, payment over time, or unusual conditions, speaking with a legal professional familiar with equine transactions is sensible.

Many sellers begin with plain-language contract *templates*, adapting them to reflect what has already been agreed. Templates are frameworks, not safeguards. They work best when the thinking behind the sale is already sound. Useful starting points include websites for:

- breed societies and registries
- state or national horse councils
- equestrian federations
- government small-business or consumer affairs
- equine industry associations

If a contract feels confusing, overly complex, or disconnected from what has been discussed, that is a signal to seek advice before proceeding. Use the following checklist as a safeguard. It ensures responsibility transfers deliberately, rather than by assumption.

Checklist: What must be settled once a sale is confirmed.

Sale confirmation

□ Sale price agreed
□ Method of sale confirmed (private treaty, subject to vet, deposit held, etc.)
□ Any conditions attached to the sale clearly stated
□ Confirmation that the horse is no longer being actively offered (if applicable)

Payment

□ Amount and timing of payment agreed
□ Deposit amount (if applicable) and whether it is refundable
□ Final payment method confirmed
□ Understanding that the horse is not sold until funds clear

Ownership and risk

□ Exact point at which ownership transfers
□ When responsibility for veterinary costs transfers
□ Insurance responsibility clarified
□ Emergency decision-making authority agreed if the horse remains on the seller's property

Collection and agistment

□ Collection date agreed or estimated
□ Agistment terms confirmed if collection is delayed
□ Agistment rate, inclusions, and payment timing stated
□ Notice period required for collection clarified

Documentation and records

□ List of documents that exist for the horse
□ Which documents will transfer to the buyer
□ When transfer will occur (immediate / after payment / after collection)
□ Who is responsible for lodging transfer paperwork
□ Any fees associated with transfers identified

Practical handover

□ Current routine, feeding, and management explained
□ Any upcoming vaccinations, shoeing, or treatments disclosed
□ Transport arrangements confirmed
□ Contact details exchanged for post-sale questions if appropriate

Serious buyers will spend much time checking horses out.

If this book has shifted the way you think about selling, even slightly, I would value you taking the time to leave a review on Amazon.

It helps other horse lovers find their way to this information, and supports better outcomes for horses overall. If you have already done so, you're awesome!

Chapter 15

Auctions and special sales

Choosing the right pathway

Up to this point, this book has focused largely on private sales, where sellers retain a high degree of control over process, timing, communication, and decision-making.

Special sales change that balance.

They introduce intermediaries, standardised conditions, compressed timelines, and, in some cases, reduced remedies for both buyer and seller. These sales can work very well. They can also magnify mistakes.

Public sales

Public and catalogue-driven sales tend to suit horses that can be understood quickly, without conversation or careful placement. They work best where the horse's role is obvious and its appeal translates easily across riders, handlers, and environments.

It is important to consider whether you are likely to be placing horses through the same sale in the future. Satisfied buyers come back seeking similar. Put your best sale horses through, rather than 'roughies' or horses you just want to be rid of. Your reputation builds if you offer good horses and set realistic reserves.

Once a horse enters an auction catalogue, much of the decision-making shifts away from the individual seller and into a predefined framework. Terms are standardised. Conditions are published. Remedies are limited. Buyers are expected to perform due diligence quickly and independently.

For sellers, auctions offer reach and momentum. Once the hammer falls, the sale is binding, subject only to the auction's stated conditions. There is usually no right of return for suitability, temperament, or future performance.

Catalogue descriptions and disclosure

Catalogue descriptions carry significant weight.

Buyers may never speak to you directly before bidding. What is written is often relied upon without further clarification. Ambiguity does not protect you here. It increases risk.

Descriptions should be factual, restrained, and accurate. Overstating ability, glossing over limitations, or using aspirational language is particularly risky in this environment. If a horse has a specific limitation, its intended use should be stated plainly.

Catalogue entries should typically include:

- Age, height, sex, and breeding
- Registration status and any outstanding paperwork
- Current level of training or competition
- What the horse is actively doing *now*
- Any material limitations that affect use
- Accurate location and inspection details

Catalogue language should describe what the horse **does**, not what it may become.

Costs beyond catalogue fees

Catalogue fees are rarely the full cost. Knowing these costs in advance allows you to build them into your decision. Depending on the sale, additional expenses may include:

- Stabling and care
- Transport to and from the venue
- Staff or strapper support
- Promotional material
- Veterinary inspections or certificates

- Insurance cover during the sale period

Choosing the right sale

Not all sales are created equal. Low-end auctions, sometimes locally referred to as dogger or kill-pen sales, exist primarily to move horses quickly and cheaply. Many horses entering these systems go directly to slaughter.

No responsible seller should consign a horse to this type of sale.

For competition, breeding, or quality riding horses, choose sales with:

- An established reputation
- Transparent conditions
- Broad or elite marketing reach
- A buyer base aligned with your horse's use

A sale platform should serve your horse, not simply move it.

Questions to ask before committing to a special sale

- Am I comfortable selling this horse without meeting the buyer?
- Is the catalogue description sufficient to protect both parties?
- Do the conditions align with my ethics and risk tolerance?
- Does this horse suit a standardised process?

If the answer to any of these is no, reconsider.

Special sales may be the ultimate for sellers as they are often the place where the right buyers are attracted and high prices are reached.

Special sales are not shortcuts. They are tools.

Breed- and discipline-specific sales

These often sit somewhere between private sale and general auction.

They attract a more targeted audience, and buyers may arrive with clearer expectations. Many of these sales carry incentives, such as wider marketing, special events for catalogued horses, such as Futurities, breeder incentives, and lucrative prize-money.

These sales work best for horses that fit the market precisely, especially if you plan to sell horses through these sales on a regular basis. Buyers come back when they are happy and know the type of stock you will present.

Withdrawal may be expensive and only be permitted upon veterinary examination.

Auctions can be a stressful time for the horse, seller and buyer

Dispersal and Estate Sales

So often these are places where bargains can be had. Buyers tend to think they can purchase quality stock at bargain basement prices, because sellers will have 'no reserves.' They may be correct.

This is because such sales are often arranged in haste, due to extenuating circumstances. In the case of a deceased person, the family may have little first-hand knowledge of the horses, or simply have no understanding of the wishes of the owner. They just want to wind up the interests of the estate quickly so they can move on with their lives without the responsibility and financial commitment to place the horses in a carefully orchestrated way.

Worse, they may just load up the horses on a truck and send them to the local auction house to await their fate. Is this what you want?

If you wish to ensure your horses are suitably re-homed upon your death, please leave clear instructions as part of your estate succession plan in writing. Better off to gift them to a personal horse friend who can utilize them or can sell them privately on your behalf for a stake in the funds, or sell them in a well-promoted dispersal sale, with clear information on each horse's history, breeding and abilities, before it becomes a 'firesale' organized by dis-interested parties.

Online auctions

Online auctions add another layer of complexity. They increase reach but remove physical interaction. Buyers rely heavily on video, documentation, and third-party information. Misinterpretation is more likely, not less.

Sellers must be disciplined about what is shown, how it is shown, and what is claimed. Once bidding begins, withdrawal is rarely possible without penalty.

Online auctions tend to suit horses with straightforward profiles and clear use cases. They are a poor match for horses that rely on feel, routine, or careful matching.

They can, however, suit sellers who do not wish to transport a horse to a central venue or who want to test the market without committing to a live auction environment. Buyers may be able to find a horse at a location near them.

Presentation and promotional material

Presentation matters in a public sale. Clean turnout, correct discipline-specific tack, and calm handling influence perception far more than many sellers realise. Dress appropriately for your breed or discipline. Buyers notice.

Your own marketing still matters.

Do not assume the sales company will do all the work for you. It may be the difference between a sale or no-sale. Have your own material available:

- Clear signage identifying your horse
- Printed or digital photos and video
- Performance records or summaries
- Registration and breeding information

Sales platforms provide exposure. They do not replace thoughtful presentation.

Being present matters

Your presence allows you to answer questions accurately, correct misunderstandings early, observe how your horse is coping, and ensure handling remains appropriate.

If you cannot be present at all times, have a knowledgeable assistant on stand-by. A horse left entirely in others' hands can be misread quickly, particularly under time pressure. At all times leave clear contact details and return times on the stall door. Be present:

- During inspections
- During pre-trials or ridden demonstrations
- On sale day
- After the sale, during handover

Pre-sale trials and demonstrations

Pre-sale demonstrations can assist buyers, but they also increase exposure and fatigue. If pre-trials are part of the sale process:

- Limit frequency
- Monitor how your horse is coping
- Show the horse doing its normal work
- Step in if stress or fatigue becomes evident
- A tired or overwhelmed horse does not sell better.
- Whenever possible, demonstrate the horse yourself or with its regular rider.

Which horses suit special sales

Not every horse belongs in a special sale. Special sales tend to suit horses that:

- have a clear, established use
- fit the market neatly
- require minimal explanation
- cope well with handling by others
- tolerate atmosphere and routine disruption
- are being sold by someone comfortable with relinquishing control

Horses that are complex, sensitive, limited, or highly dependent on rider fit are often better served by private sale.

Reserve prices and unknown buyers

One of the defining features of auction is that you do not choose the buyer. A reserve should reflect the price at which you are genuinely willing to part with your horse, knowing you may never meet the buyer. If that thought causes hesitation, auction may not be the right pathway for you.

If the hammer falls at or above your reserve, the horse is sold.

Your relationship with the auctioneer

The auctioneer's responsibility is to you, the vendor, not the buyer. Ask how the horse will be introduced in the ring and whether you may speak with the auctioneer beforehand.

Provide the auctioneer with accurate information about your horse *in advance*, including significant bloodlines and any limitations or sensitivities that affect handling or presentation.

Many sellers choose to be present at the auctioneer's box when their horse sells. This allows last-minute clarifications and ensures nothing material is misunderstood.

Presentation in the ring

Dress appropriately for your breed or discipline. Use correct tack. Keep handling calm and familiar. Breathe!

Where possible, lead or present your own horse. You will be time restricted, so have a plan before you enter the ring. For example, if you state it is a good children's pony, you might allow a child to ride it in bareback. You know it best. You know how it stands, walks, responds, and settles. You know what to avoid and what shows it to advantage.

Do not leave this to the sales company or a generic handler unless you have no alternative.

Auction dynamics

Auctioneers are engaged by the sale company. Their primary responsibility is to conduct the sale efficiently, in accordance with the published conditions and in the interests of the vendor body as a whole.

Common dynamics sellers should be aware of:

Auctions move quickly, and momentum matters. The handler should **listen carefully** to the bidding. If bidding slows, he can change his approach by demonstrating something else to stir up the bidding. This can be done for example, by trotting the horse out, getting on and off, riding it bareback, showing tricks the horse knows, picking up legs, rubbing ears, ground tie or cracking a stockwhip. Anything extra the horse knows. So think about that in advance.

In this environment:

- bids may be encouraged with language designed to keep the sale moving
- hesitation may be framed as opportunity
- silence may be interpreted as lack of interest rather than uncertainty

None of this is improper. It is how auctions function.

What matters is that you enter the ring knowing:

- your reserve
- your position if the reserve is not met
- and your willingness (or not) to sell if bidding stops there

Success! When pedigree, conformation, training, promotion and presentation come together

Chapter 16

After the hammer falls

What happens next

The moment the hammer falls is decisive. What often causes confusion is that legal transfer and physical possession do not happen at the same moment.

What changes at the fall of the hammer

Once your horse is sold at auction:

- You no longer control the sale
- You do not manage insurance or transport
- You rely on the auction's conditions to carry the sale through
- That moment marks the legal sale, subject to the auction's published terms.

From that point, in most auctions:

- Ownership transfers
- Risk usually transfers to the buyer
- Insurance responsibility typically shifts immediately

However, the horse does not usually leave the grounds at that exact moment. This is where misunderstandings can arise.

Care between sale and collection

Although ownership and risk often transfer at the fall of the hammer, the horse usually remains on site for a short period. Try to be available after the sale for a handover with the buyer. You may have questions and he may want to know more about the horse's background. It is appropriate to exchange contact details. Don't rely on the agents to give you this information in a timely manner.

During this time:

- The auction company (or their contractors) provides basic care
- This typically includes feeding, watering, stabling, and routine supervision
- That care is provided **on behalf of the buyer**, not the seller

This is a holding arrangement. It is not an extension of the sale and not a trial period.

The scope and duration of this care are set out in the auction's conditions.

Insurance After the Sale

In most auction sales:

- Buyers are expected to insure immediately
- Many auction houses recommend insurance be in place before bidding
- Some offer short-term cover through a nominated insurer, at the buyer's cost

Do not assume your existing insurance continues once the hammer falls. Many policies cease automatically upon transfer of ownership.

If a buyer fails to insure, they are assuming that risk themselves.

Transport and collection

Responsibility for arranging transport almost always sits with the buyer. Auction conditions will specify:

- How long the horse may remain on site
- When stabling or agistment fees begin
- Penalties or consequences if collection is delayed

Caution for sellers

While conditions may state that risk transfers at the fall of the hammer, practical responsibility does not always feel so clean.

If a horse becomes ill, injured, or distressed while still physically on site, disputes can arise quickly around supervision, timing, reporting and authority for veterinary decisions.

Before consigning a horse, make sure you understand:

- Exactly when risk transfers
- Who authorises veterinary treatment if required
- Who is notified if something goes wrong
- If any part of this is unclear, ask before entering the horse.

If the buyer defaults on payment

Auction sales feel final, but payment still matters. If the buyer fails to settle within the time frame set out, the sale does not simply resolve itself.

What happens next

The auction company will usually notify you, apply the default provisions and advise whether the horse will be re-offered, sold privately, or withdrawn.

Some sales allow you to accept the default and retain the horse, authorise resale at the buyer's risk, or negotiate a private-treaty outcome. Others do not.

In some cases, the auctioneer may approach the under-bidder to offer them the opportunity to purchase the horse, usually under the original sale conditions and often at the final bid price. Be aware:

- The under-bidder is not obliged to proceed
- A fresh agreement may be required
- Payment, risk transfer, and timelines reset once a new sale is confirmed
- Check whether resale costs or shortfalls can be recovered

Important: Do not argue with a default, improvise solutions or release the horse.

What happens next is governed almost entirely by the sale company's published terms. In most auctions:

- The buyer is in breach of contract
- The auctioneer acts on behalf of the vendor
- Remedies are determined by the sale conditions, not informal goodwill

Common consequences may include:

- Forfeiture of the buyer's deposit
- Liability for interest, penalties, or resale costs
- The horse being re-offered
- The buyer being barred from future sales

Responsibility during a default

Until payment is completed and ownership transfers under the auction conditions, responsibility usually remains with you or with the sale company acting on your behalf. This typically means:

- You remain responsible for the horse's welfare
- Feeding, watering, and stabling continue under sale arrangements
- Insurance should remain in place
- The horse must not be released

Never allow a horse to leave the sale grounds until:

- Full payment has cleared
- Sale confirmation has been issued
- Responsibility has formally transferred

When something goes wrong, the auction structure is what keeps the situation contained for you and for your horse.

A buyer cannot return the horse due to unsuitability or because he has changed his mind. If a horse is misrepresented, even through no fault of the seller, such as DNA testing resulting in an unproven pedigree, a horse substitution, or mismatch to ID, this becomes a legal matter to resolve, not that of the auction company or the registration body.

Chapter 17

After the sale

The reality of letting go

The moment the horse leaves you, something shifts. For the buyer, the relationship is only just beginning.

For the seller, the transaction may feel complete, yet the emotional and practical consequences of how the sale was handled continue quietly in the background.

But how a sale ends matters just as much as how it begins. Not because you owe anything beyond what was agreed, but because endings shape reputation, memory, and trust in ways that last far longer than the sale itself.

Follow up without entanglement

Most buyers have the courtesy to let you know that the horse has arrived and settled in. A brief, thoughtful follow-up after the sale if you don't hear anything, is often appreciated.

A simple message checking that the horse arrived safely, or wishing the buyer well, reinforces professionalism and care. It acknowledges the transition without reopening the transaction.

Once ownership has transferred, responsibility has transferred with it.

Asking for updates occasionally is reasonable if the relationship supports it. Expecting regular reports or inserting yourself into decisions is not.

We try to maintain a relationship with buyers such that if we have heard nothing, we will reach out in 6 or 12 months, just to ascertain progress and indicate interest in that journey.

We enjoy receiving updates, photos, or competition results as this is feedback, and can be used in promotional material.

The healthiest post sale relationships are those where goodwill exists without obligation. Many buyers become wonderful friends and we are blessed to know them.

Another excellent sign of goodwill is to offer equipment, such as a bridle or rugs which fit the horse in question, at the time of sale. This is usually an appreciated gesture.

There is the odd occasion where a buyers does not wish to have it revealed that they are the buyer. This maybe due to timing, or personal matters. We once had a buyer whose ex-partner was on a restraining order. If a buyer prefers privacy after purchase, please respect it, regardless of whether you know the reason.

As a breeder, I will always suggest that if a resale is necessary in the future, we are prepared to assist with advertising through our channels and in some instances take the horse back, either for breeding purposes or resale.

Horse Records

All our horses are maintained and recorded on the HorseRecords programme which I recommend. The beauty of this programme is that it can track every horse, their feeding, excercise and health schedules, pedigree and background of the horse, progeny, files and photos *all in the one place.* At the click of a button, you can transfer all this information to the new owner, at the same time keeping it archived for your own records.

Here is the link:https://www.horserecords.info/accounts/login/

The HorseRecords programme - it's free to trial for the first two horses.

Education, support, and optional after-sale contact

If you choose to provide educational material, recommendations, or transitional guidance, frame it as support. Buyers who feel empowered rather than supervised are more likely to succeed and more likely to speak positively about their experience.

This can include breed printed material, membership forms, guides and current routines, to aim for the smooth transition.

In some cases, sellers may offer post sale support, particularly where a horse has specific management needs or where the buyer is stepping into unfamiliar territory.

This support should always be optional, time limited, and clearly defined.

You can offer help where it is useful but advice imposed becomes interference. Handled well, the handover prevents doubt or unresolved emotion from carrying forward into later decisions.

Regret, second thoughts, and changing your mind

You may experience regret after a sale. We've all felt it. It is especially common when a horse was deeply loved, when circumstances forced the sale, or when the future feels uncertain.

Regret does not mean the sale was wrong. It means the relationship mattered.

What is not acceptable is acting on that regret in ways that destabilise the buyer or the horse.

If regret arises, sit with it privately. Speak to someone neutral. Reflect on whether the discomfort is about the buyer, or about your own attachment.

If there were genuine concerns about suitability that you ignored earlier, that is information to learn from, not grounds to intervene.

Certainty must come before the sale, not after.

Reputation travels quietly. Your reputation is not built through volume. It is built through consistency.

> *It takes 20 years to build a reputation and five minutes to ruin it. If you think about that, you will do things differently.* – Warren Buffett

Buyers remember how they were treated after money changed hands. Trainers and professionals notice how sellers speak about completed transactions.

Word travels without fanfare.

Sellers often underestimate how much their post sale behaviour is noticed. A seller who handles endings with grace becomes someone others are comfortable dealing with. A seller who becomes intrusive, resentful, controlling or unpredictable after a sale creates hesitation around future transactions.

Closure matters

Every sale deserves a sense of closure.

For the buyer, that may come through settling into a new routine. For the seller, it may come through reflection, documentation, or simply acknowledging that a chapter has ended.

When those responsibilities are met thoughtfully from beginning to end, the sale does more than transfer ownership. It holds together well.

When good horses go wrong.

How mismatches develop quietly

Example 1. The quiet schoolmaster who became difficult

The horse was advertised as quiet, reliable, and suitable for most riders. In its previous home, it lived in a paddock with two other horses. It was brought in for work four days a week in the arena and taken out for a relaxed trail ride once a week. Its routine was predictable, social, and balanced.

The new owner agisted privately. The horse was kept stabled and day-yarded alone. Work consisted of two arena sessions a week with an instructor and two additional days of prolonged lunging.
Over time, the horse became increasingly excitable in the arena and resistant to leaving the property. What had once been described as sensible began to look anxious and barn sour.

Nothing fundamental had changed about the horse. The environment had. The horse was no longer living or working in a way that supported its temperament. A routine that once kept it settled had been replaced with isolation, increased pressure, and reduced variety. The behaviour was not misrepresentation. It was mismatch.

Example 2. The competition horse without a competition life

A horse advertised as experienced and straightforward at competition level had been produced with frequent outings, professional support, and a rider comfortable managing atmosphere.

The buyer planned to compete, but outings became infrequent. The horse spent long periods between events and was ridden primarily at home by a less experienced rider. Exposure decreased. Pressure increased.

At the next competition, the horse felt sharp and unsettled. The buyer questioned whether the horse had truly been as experienced as advertised.
In reality, the horse had lost the context that made it reliable. Experience does not exist in isolation. It is maintained through repetition and familiarity.

Example 3. The capable horse ridden below its needs

A horse described as safe and forgiving had been ridden consistently by a confident rider who maintained clear boundaries and expectations.
The new owner rode infrequently and cautiously, often avoiding moments of resistance rather than addressing them. Over time, the horse began to test limits, not out of malice, but confusion.

The buyer felt misled. The horse felt unclear. What was missing was not honesty, but connection between the rider the horse had been shaped by and the rider now sitting on its back.

Example 4. The impulsive purchase that moved too fast

A buyer felt an immediate connection and pushed to proceed quickly. The seller, relieved by the enthusiasm, allowed the process to accelerate.

Vet checks were minimal. Advice was deferred. The buyer later realised the horse required more management and skill than anticipated. Regret followed quickly. The mismatch was not discovered at the viewing, but after the sale. It was created by haste.

Example 5. The fearful buyer who rushed to secure the horse

Another buyer had missed out previously and felt pressure to act. They overlooked small hesitations, dismissed their own questions, and committed before fully understanding the horse's needs.

Once the horse arrived, anxiety replaced excitement. Small issues felt large. Confidence eroded. Fear drove the purchase, and fear followed it home.

What these mismatches have in common

In each case, the horse was not wrong. The buyer was not careless. The seller was not necessarily dishonest. The problem was context.

What sellers can do to reduce this risk

Sellers cannot control what happens after the sale, but they can help set realistic expectations:

- describe not just what the horse does, but how it lives
- explain what keeps the horse settled and functional
- slow down buyers who want to move too quickly
- name where changes in routine may matter

Many behaviour problems which buyers attribute to temperament or suspicions of drugging, are actually responses to change.

The emptiness you feel when you have traded your good mate for a cheque.

A guide for new owners

It gives a sense of professionalism if you have something in print to give to the new owner. Here is a basic template you can use to make up your own 2-4 page Guide.

Your new horse. A practical guide for the first weeks:

Horse's name: ______________________________
Date of sale: ______________________________
Seller: ______________________________
Phone: ______________________________
Email: ______________________________

Welcome
Congratulations on your new horse.
The first few days in a new home can feel unsettled for both horse and owner.
A change of environment, feed, companions, and routine is a lot to take in.
It does take some horses a few months to settle in well.
This guide simply outlines the horse's current management and a few practical suggestions to help the transition go smoothly.
Nothing complicated. Just the small details that make life easier.

Current daily routine
Horses settle best when their routine stays familiar. If possible, keep feeding and management similar for the first week or two before making changes. If you plan to change feeds or increase work, do so gradually. A quiet start allows the horse time to settle physically and mentally into the new environment.
Morning
• Feed: ______________________________
• Hay: ______________________________
• Turnout: ______________________________
Midday
• ______________________________
Evening
• Feed: ______________________________
• Stabled or paddock: ______________________________
Water
• Trough / bucket / automatic: ______________________________

Exercise and work
Current workload
• ______________________________
Usual type of work
• ______________________________
Days per week
• ______________________________

Notes
• ______________________________

Feed and supplements

Current feed
• ______________________________
Hard feed amounts
• ______________________________
Supplements or additives
• ______________________________
Salt or minerals
• ______________________________
Sudden feed changes are one of the most common causes of stress and digestive upset. Introduce any new feed slowly over 7 to 10 days.

Health and management records

Worming
• Last done: ________________
• Product used: ________________
• Next due: ________________
Vaccinations
• ________________
Dentistry
• Last done: ________________
Farrier
• Interval: ________________
• Last done: ________________
Clipping, rugging, special care
• ________________
Usual veterinary clinic
Name: ________________
Phone: ________________

What this horse is used to

These small details help prevent misunderstandings.
• Used to being caught daily
• Comfortable tied up
• Leads quietly
• Loads and travels well
• Used to dogs / children / machinery
• Prefers company / happy alone
• Sensitive to sudden feed changes
• Other notes: ______________________________

Settling into a new home

Most horses adjust quickly, but a little patience at the beginning goes a long way.

For the first week or two:
- Keep feed similar to current ration
- Maintain a consistent daily routine
- Avoid sudden changes in workload
- Introduce new horses gradually over a fence first
- Expect mild stress or reduced appetite initially
- Allow time to observe before asking too much

A quiet, steady approach usually works best. Settling is a process, not an event.

Registration and breed information

Breed organisation
- ____________________

Transfer of ownership
- ____________________

Membership or resources
- ____________________

Websites or contacts
- ____________________

Paperwork and reminders

You may wish to arrange:
□ Transfer of registration
□ Insurance
□ Farrier booking
□ Dental check, due 2x annually
□ Worming schedule noted
□ Feed transition plan

Staying in touch

If you ever have questions, or simply want to let us know how things are going, you are always welcome to get in touch.
We like to hear how our horses are settling into their new homes.
Phone: ____________________
Email: ____________________

Final note

This horse has been raised and managed with care. Small, thoughtful steps make the biggest difference.
We hope you enjoy a wonderful partnership ahead.

Saying goodbye, a breeder's dilemma

Chapter 18

Real seller experiences

And how to avoid their mistakes

Scenario 1. Seller 'improves' the horse

A few years ago a client bought a horse from us for a film about outback Australia. He needed quality horses for the lead horseman. Tough horses. Horses that actually looked like they belonged in the bush.

He was to collect ours after picking up another horse. “Where is the other horse?” I asked.

He rolled his eyes. “The stupid girl decided to body clip it so it ‘looked nice.’ With only six weeks to go before filming I couldn’t take it. It pisses me off.”

The horse was meant to look like an outback horse, a working horse, not a freshly clipped show hunter. Six weeks is not enough time to grow a coat back.

And this happens more often than people realise.

I have bought horses and had them arrive with the mane clipped off. Gone. Helping? Not quite.

If that horse is destined for the show ring you have just wiped out an entire season while the mane grows back. If that horse is to be turned out into a paddock, it needs its mane!

Good intentions. Wrong result. The rule is simple.

If the buyer did not ask for it, do not do it.

Scenario 2. When the pedigree is wrong

A friend of mine used to drive past a well known warmblood stud regularly and noticed a youngster standing in the paddock. It looked like quite a nice type, although it was thin, wormy, and clearly not thriving.

Eventually curiosity got the better of her and she stopped to ask about it. Yes, it was for sale, and for a little under market price. The stud explained they were selling the foal on behalf of a client.

The pedigree sounded impressive, but something did not add up. The foal was the wrong colour for the mating they described. When she raised the question, she was reassured that everything was correct as they had inseminated the mare themselves.

So she bought the youngster.

When the time came to collect it, more problems became obvious. The foal was unhandled, frightened of everything, and the question about its parentage had still not been properly resolved.

Eventually she arranged DNA testing.

The results showed that neither the recorded sire nor the recorded dam could be the parents!

The stud had mixed up two mares belonging to the same owner and assigned the foal to the paperwork of the wrong mare. This meant the youngster was unable to be registered, as the correct dam was unregistered.

Pedigree matters. Records matter. If you are selling a horse, particularly a young horse, the parentage must be correct and verified. Otherwise you are not selling a pedigree. You are selling a guess.

Scenario 3. When you lose track of horses

We once sold four fillies to an elderly man who intended breeding from them. Only after the sale did we discover he planned to put them in foal as two year olds. That was the first thing that went wrong. After they left we lost track of them for many years.

Then one day we received a phone call from a man asking about the name and breeding of one of the horses. He had recognised our brand and wanted the pedigree. He declined to give his name and hung up.

Less than half an hour later the old buyer rang. He was furious. He accused us of helping someone who had “stolen his horses” and demanded information so he could track them down. Of course we knew nothing about it, and with that sort of attitude we were not exactly inspired to help him either.

A few years passed before the next call came. This time it was a young woman who said she had been given two of the mares as broodmares from the old man, because he was in poor health. I asked her directly whether the horses had been stolen. She said they had managed to recover two of them, but the other two were still missing.

The mares she had were unbroken and barely handled. Only one had ever produced a foal, which she now had. She promised to keep in touch.

The very next day another anonymous call arrived. This man wanted the breeding details for mare number three. He told me she had already produced several foals for him. I gave him the pedigree, but mentioned we had heard the mares might have been stolen.

His reply was blunt.

"I paid for this mare fair and square from a stockman who said he was given her as payment for a debt."

Then he hung up.

Several years later the story surfaced again when a friend rang to say she had bought two elderly mares from a newspaper advertisement. They were thin and ageing, but she hoped to get a final foal from each before her own stallion died. She recognised them from our brand.

Once again I explained the rather tangled history of those mares. (She did eventually manage to breed a filly from each of them.)

And no sooner had I put the phone down than the old man rang again, still angry, still accusing us of helping strangers who had 'stolen his horses.' I told him it had been years since we had last heard from him. All I ever wanted was to locate them and understand what had actually happened.

I have no idea what story he had been given about us or by whom. (His details were publicly listed through the society records.) He hung up on me. And that was the last we ever heard of him.

The truth is we never discovered the full story. The mares had clearly passed through several hands, sometimes through sales, sometimes through debts, sometimes through circumstances that were never fully explained. Each person believed they had acquired the horses legitimately, yet the original owner believed they had been taken from him.

Situations like this remind you how easily horses can disappear once they leave your property. Without proper records, clear communication, and responsible ownership, a horse's history can become surprisingly tangled.

For breeders and sellers it reinforces an important lesson. Once a horse leaves your hands, you may not always control what happens next.

All you can do is sell responsibly, keep accurate records, and hope the people who buy your horses treat them with the same care and honesty that you would.

Scenario 4. Horse lands in the wrong home

We once sold a very nice two year old gelding. He was broken in, quiet, and sensible, although naturally still green as any young horse would be. He sold to a home about 1000 kilometres away and the initial reports after he arrived were all positive.

Three weeks later we received a phone call.

The owner told us she was sending the horse back and expected a full refund.

The problem, apparently, was her Shetland ponies. She kept them rugged with full hoods and all the trimmings. Our young horse had never seen anything like that in his life and was absolutely terrified of them. Because of this she said he would not settle and she did not want him, that we had misled her that he was quiet.

We suggested she give him a little more time. A young horse often needs a period of adjustment when he arrives somewhere new. But she would not consider it.

Reluctantly we agreed to refund the money, although we were under no obligation to do so. She paid the transport to send him home and the horse came back to us.

As it turned out, that was the best thing that could have happened to him.

About six weeks later he sold again, this time to a young girl who schooled him entirely herself. Over the following years that horse went on to win many junior and open competitions in a wide range of disciplines, often at the highest level. A few years later she even won a high point saddle at our National Championships with him.

People constantly commented on how quiet and reliable he was. It just proves a point that every horse breeder learns sooner or later:

One person's problem horse can easily become someone else's champion.

Scenario 5. Why a sales contract matters

A friend sold a foal and for the first year or so they heard nothing but glowing reports about him. Everything sounded wonderful. The horse was progressing well and they seemed very happy.

About eighteen months later they saw her at a show for the first time since the sale.

She was trying to load the horse into a float and it was not going well. The youngster absolutely refused to go in. As it was raining the tailboard was slippery and he kept losing his footing, sliding backwards and even falling right over onto his back a couple of times.

Before I had the chance to step in and offer assistance, another person intervened and helped her. The horse was eventually taken home.

About three months later they received a phone call.

They were told the horse had "wobbles" and that this condition was likely genetic. Therefore, in her view, she had purchased a faulty horse and wanted a replacement.

The breeder explained that it was very unlikely to be genetic and reminded her that I had seen the horse fall heavily while loading at the show. It seemed far more likely that the problem had developed after that incident.

She was not satisfied and became quite insistent.

At that point they sought legal advice. The lawyer told them they had no obligation to replace the horse, but suggested that taking the horse back might be the simplest way to protect their reputation.

Unfortunately they only had one similar horse available at the time, a filly they had actually intended to keep themselves. Reluctantly they offered her that filly.

Six weeks later they heard from a neighbour that she had sold the filly. There was no phone call. No offer to return her. No communication at all. When asked where the filly had gone she refused to say. The breeder was understandably very angry.

The explanation was that the filly was "too much like the gelding" and she could not cope emotionally with that.

Experiences like this teach you a very important lesson.

Always have a clear sales contract. It should state exactly what happens if a horse is returned, exchanged, or resold. Without that protection, even well-intentioned decisions can come back to bite you later.

Scenario 6. Buyer integrity

Most sellers could give you a few instances where they had 'bad' sales due to people misrepresenting their ability or their intention to do the right thing with a good horse. Lots of talk about their plans and then nothing happens. This is most frustrating.

Probably the worst instance for a friend was a beautiful well-bred gelding sold to a dressage woman in Adelaide. After a few months she rang to complain about this horse's attitude and how hopeless he was. The friend said to send him straight back and they would refund his price. He arrived and he was just a mental wreck.

He was a heartbroken horse, that had completely lost all faith in people.

The friend handled it for two days and decided to put this lovely horse down. Horses are so forgiving but this fellow would have taken ages to learn to be a happy horse again so they made the call.

After putting him down, her husband made a very fierce announcement "You are NOT to sell another one of our horses to any woman from Adelaide"

Scenario 7. Nerve-wracking sale overseas

From a stud manager: The late 1970s were a very difficult time for horse prices. Markets were depressed and many breeders were simply trying to move horses and keep cash flow going. During that period we had a couple of dealings with buyers from Thailand, which opened the door to one of the most nerve-wracking sales we ever made.

Transport logistics were very different then. There were no regular livestock flights to rely on. Instead, we had to wait for a Flying Tiger cargo plane to arrive in Melbourne or Sydney with space available. Until one appeared, everything sat in limbo.

An order eventually came through for a group of 10 small, fast horses. They had to be unbranded and quick, suitable for being registered as locally bred and raced in the popular unregistered meetings in Thailand at the time. Because the market was so depressed, suitable horses could be purchased quite cheaply, particularly those that were a little undersized.

We gathered a small group and waited for confirmation of transport. Payment was arranged through a Letter of Credit, which in those days could take weeks to finalise.

Then the phone rang. A Flying Tiger plane had unexpectedly landed in Melbourne. It would be leaving again within twenty-four hours and had room for the horses.

The problem was obvious. Payment had not yet cleared, and in the late 1970s there was no way to rush international banking. We were faced with a decision. Either miss the flight and potentially lose the sale, or send the horses without payment.

After some hurried phone calls we managed to contact the senior military officer who was organising the purchase. The best he could offer was his personal assurance that the money would be waiting if we loaded the horses.

An emergency discussion was held and we decided to take the gamble. The horses had not cost a great deal, and sometimes in the horse business you simply have to back your judgement.

Transport was organised immediately. The horses were collected and taken to

Melbourne from South Australia, and despite feeling dreadful with the flu, our representative insisted on going with them. He was not about to watch a load of unpaid horses leave the country without being present.

The Flying Tiger arrived around midnight in Bangkok and parked in a remote corner of the airport. Trucks were waiting. The horses were quickly unloaded onto the trucks, and vanished into the night.

And just like that, he was left standing on the tarmac.

With no contact and still battling the flu, he eventually made his way into the city and found a small hotel room. Several anxious days passed with no real communication, only vague reassurances that payment would be waiting when he departed.

Finally it was time to leave.

At the airport he was approached and handed a brown paper bag. Inside were thousands of dollars in used Australian fifty-dollar notes.

The relief was quickly replaced by another worry. Carrying that amount of cash through an international airport was hardly ideal. Fearing the money might disappear before he even left the country, he headed to the nearest restroom and hid the notes wherever he could. Boots, pockets, clothing, anywhere they would fit.

It was quite a sight when he arrived back in Australia. As he waddled into the terminal looking distinctly larger than when he had left, the first comment was that he appeared to have put on weight while away. "Let's just get out of here," came the urgent reply.

The reason became obvious once we reached the car and he began pulling bundles of fifty-dollar notes from boots, pockets, and every other hiding place.

Looking back now it seems almost unbelievable. It certainly would not happen that way today. But at the time it was simply part of doing business in a difficult market, and it remains one of the most nerve-wracking horse sales we ever undertook.

That sale says a great deal about how the horse business once operated. Transactions were often built more on reputation and personal assurances than on the layers of contracts and safeguards that exist today. It was certainly a risk to let those horses leave the country without payment in hand. Yet in difficult markets decisions sometimes had to be made quickly, and opportunities did not wait for perfect circumstances. Judgement, experience, and a sense of the people involved carried a great deal of weight.

That does not mean such risks should be taken lightly. Modern banking systems, international transport arrangements, and traceable payments have removed much of the uncertainty that once surrounded overseas sales. Still its a reminder that the horse trade has always involved a balance between caution and courage. Sometimes you play it safe. Occasionally you take a calculated gamble and hope your reading of the situation is correct.

Scenario 7. Selling a green-broke gelding

From Jane: I was selling my Arabian gelding. He was registered and green broke, and I priced him accordingly. I had an interested buyer who said he wanted the horse, but he could only afford $3,000. I was willing to negotiate, so that part was not an issue.

However, he said he did not want to pay for the horse until after a six month trial. He also could not afford transport and asked if I would drive the horse six hours toward him so it would be easier for him to collect.

At that point I told him I would not sell him the horse.

He responded by telling me I was the worst person ever and I needed to explain to his 24 year old autistic brother why I would not sell him his dream horse to learn on.

Are you ready to sell?

Chapter 19

Ready enough

What if I don't feel ready?

There is a moment that comes just before you offer a horse for sale that very few people talk about.

On the surface, everything looks ready. The horse is standing there, healthy and well handled. The work has been done. You know its history, its temperament, its strengths and its limits. Yet instead of feeling decisive, you may feel something else entirely.

A quiet pause. A second-guessing. A subtle thought that says, maybe I'm not quite ready yet. Not ready to advertise. Not ready to speak to strangers. Not ready to answer questions with authority. Not ready to ask for real money.

It rarely feels like fear. It feels sensible. Responsible, even. You tell yourself you will just wait a little longer, do one more thing, fix one more small detail. Another week becomes another month, and sometimes another year.

The horse is ready. The seller is the one holding back.

This is far more common than most people admit, especially among thoughtful, ethical owners who care deeply about doing things properly. Ironically, the very people who are most prepared are often the least convinced of it.

Why readiness rarely feels like confidence

Many people assume that confidence is the sign they are ready. They expect a feeling of certainty to arrive first, some inner signal that says, now you know enough, now you can step forward. In reality, it almost never works like that.

In horses, confidence is usually built after the fact, not before it. I learned this long before I ever sold a horse, when I was starting my own young stock.

As a teenager I had very little in the way of facilities. No arena, no round yard, nothing elaborate or purpose-built. If I was breaking one in, it was usually out in the open using a lunge line, because that was simply what I had.

By modern standards it sounds terribly basic.

But those early experiences taught me something important. By the time I ever put a saddle on a youngster, the real work had already been done. I had handled those foals and young horses for 2-3 years. They were caught, led, tied up, groomed, washed, rugged and handled all over their bodies. They understood pressure and release. They trusted me, and I trusted them.

Backing and mouthing were not dramatic milestones. They were simply the next small steps in a long process that had started when they were very young. I did not feel especially brave or talented. I did not feel like an expert. I simply knew it was OK to take the next step without trepidation or fanfare.

I had belief in myself!

That quiet understanding, not confidence, is what made it work. Selling horses is much the same.

It is easy to look around and assume you need better facilities, more experience, or a more professional image before you try to sell. A bigger property. A smarter set-up. More years behind you. Those things may be helpful, but they are not the deciding factor.

A well handled, honestly represented horse shown by a steady, thoughtful seller will always inspire more trust than a glossy advertisement backed by uncertainty. When you strip it back, readiness is not an emotional state. It is practical.

For the horse, readiness means that what you are offering matches reality. The horse can do what you say it can do. It behaves consistently. It has been handled thoroughly and safely. There are no surprises waiting for the buyer on the day.

For you, readiness means you understand the horse clearly. You can describe it honestly. You know its strengths and you are not hiding its limitations.

You have thought through how you will show it, how you will answer questions, and how you will protect both the horse and the buyer with sensible agreements. None of this is glamorous. It is simply groundwork. You already know more than you think

Just like those early years with my youngsters, it is the quiet preparation that makes the bigger step feel almost uneventful.

Another trap for sellers is comparison

There will always be someone with a bigger stud, fancier facilities, or a louder presence. It is easy to assume that those people must know more, and that you should wait until you reach their level before putting yourself forward. But buyers are not looking for the most impressive operation. If you've followed what I have written you know they are looking for someone they can *trust*.

Someone calm. Someone clear. Someone honest. They want to deal with the person who knows that particular horse best.

And that person is you.

You have fed it in the dark, watched it grow through awkward stages, noticed small changes in temperament, seen what unsettles it and what settles it. You know the details no one else could possibly know.

That knowledge is not theoretical. It is lived. It is exactly what a buyer needs. You do not have to be the expert on all horses.

You only need to be the expert on this one.

The quiet signs you are already ready

In the horse world, people are careful about who they trust. They do not casually hand over their time, their children, or their animals to someone they consider inexperienced. So when people start asking your opinion, that tells you something.

When they ask you to look over a young horse, or to help them choose between two prospects, or to explain feeding, handling or bitting, they are already placing confidence in your judgement. They have quietly decided that you know more than they do.

Long before you feel like an authority, others are already treating you as one.

Selling is simply an extension of that same trust.

If people respect your horses, ask about them, and recommend you to others, you are not starting from nothing. You have already built credibility through years of steady, consistent work.

You just may not have acknowledged it yet.

Taking the first steps anyway

There comes a point when only action will move you forward.

Your first advertisement may feel uncomfortable. Your first visitor may make you feel exposed. Your first negotiation may feel awkward.

That is normal.

Everything feels unfamiliar the first time. After a few sales, it becomes routine. You learn the common questions. You recognise genuine buyers more quickly. You trust your own judgement about when a match feels right or wrong.

But you only learn those things by *doing* them. Just as you cannot learn to start young horses by reading alone, you cannot learn to sell by waiting until you feel completely confident.

At some point, you simply take the next step. Not recklessly. Not carelessly. Just because the foundations are already in place.

Ready enough *is* enough

Good sellers are the ones who have quietly done the work. They have prepared their horses properly. They speak plainly. They represent their animals honestly. They think about safety and fairness for everyone involved.

From the outside, it looks effortless. From the inside, it is simply the result of many small, sensible decisions made over time. Readiness is preparation, not a feeling.

So very often, you are already further along than you think.

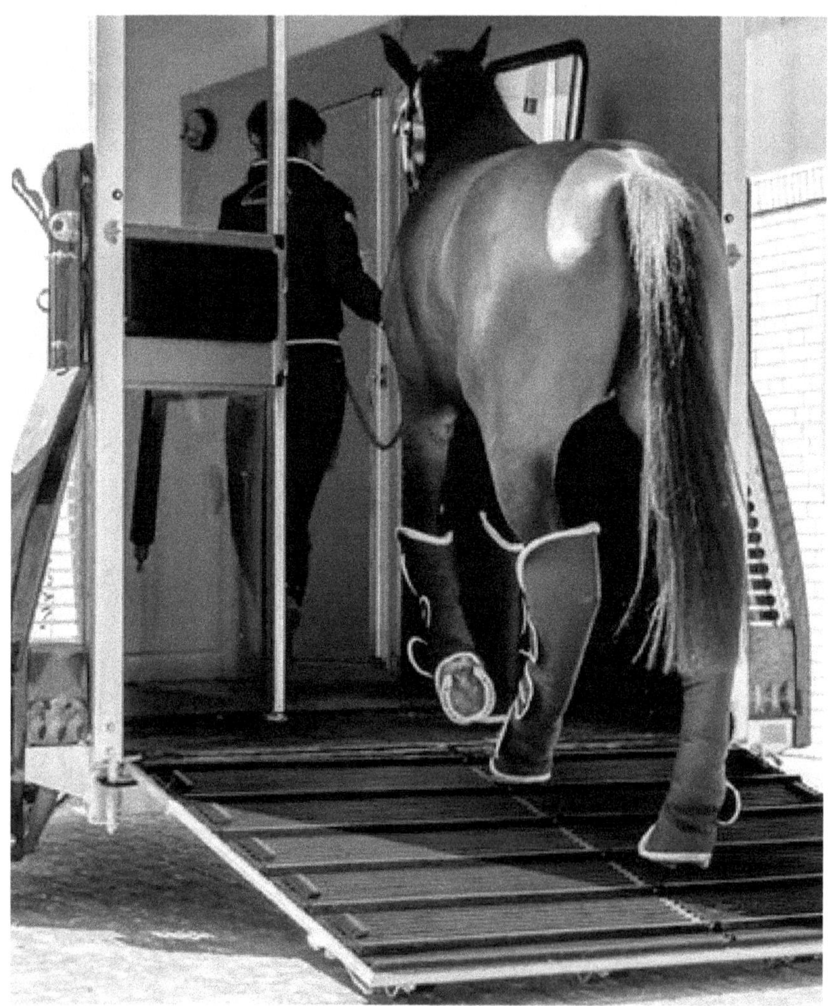

When your horse leaves and a big part of your life goes with it.

Chapter 20

When selling is not the answer

The decisions that define your standards

There are moments in horse ownership where selling is not the right answer.

This is uncomfortable to say in a book about selling horses, but it is essential. Responsibility does not end with finding a buyer. In some cases, responsibility means choosing not to sell at all.

The hardest decisions are rarely about money. They are about acknowledging limits. Some horses should not be sold into the open market.

Horses that are neglected, severely compromised, aged, or debilitated are not made safer by passing through auction houses, online sales, or loosely defined "rescues". In many cases, these pathways increase risk rather than reduce it.

Selling such horses as companions, paddock ornaments, or "projects for the right person" often shifts the burden without solving the problem. It asks someone else to absorb responsibility the original owner is unwilling or unable to carry.

That is not placement. It is avoidance.

The misuse of rescues and secondary markets

Not all rescue pathways are unethical, but they are often misunderstood.

Passing a horse into a rescue does not remove responsibility unless that organisation has the capacity, governance, and resources to manage the horse appropriately. Auctioning neglected horses under the banner of rescue rarely improves welfare outcomes.

Once control is relinquished, the horse's future becomes unpredictable.

Good intentions do not protect vulnerable horses.

Companion animals and false solutions

Offering aged or unsound horses as companions can be appropriate in limited circumstances. Too often, however, it is used to avoid making a harder decision.

A companion horse still requires care, shelter, farriery, veterinary support, and management. When these needs are beyond what the current owner is willing to provide, transferring the horse does not solve the problem.

It delays it.

The responsibility of timely euthanasia

Euthanasia is not a failure of ownership. In many cases, it is the final act of care.

The most important responsibility you have is not to sell a horse at all costs. It is to prevent suffering.

Waiting too long, hoping circumstances will change, or attempting to find "someone else" often results in urgency rather than dignity. Horses suffer most when decisions are made too late.

Better a horse is put to sleep before suffering becomes inevitable than after pain, neglect, or crisis has already taken hold. This decision should be made calmly, with veterinary guidance, and without shame.

This is not failure. It is stewardship.

Choosing integrity over convenience

Selling horses ethically sometimes means walking away from money. Sometimes it means saying no to a buyer. Sometimes it means acknowledging that the right outcome does not involve a sale.

A good sale places a horse well. A responsible owner recognises when placement is not the answer.

A final word

This book has been about doing things properly. Not quickly. Not cheaply. Not defensively.

Selling horses well requires judgement, clarity, restraint, and courage. Sometimes the most ethical decision you will make is not about who to sell to, but whether to sell at all. That decision defines your standards more than any contract ever will.

Selling horses well is not about mastering a process. It is about judgement.

Throughout this book, you have been asked to slow down moments that are often rushed, to question assumptions that are usually taken for granted, and to recognise where restraint does more good than enthusiasm.

There are many ways to sell a horse. Some are efficient. Some are profitable. Some are convenient.

Not all are responsible.

Responsibility is not measured by how quickly a horse leaves your property or how little discomfort you feel in the process. It is measured by whether the decisions you made still sit comfortably with you once the outcome is no longer in your control.

This includes knowing when to sell, how to sell, and, just as importantly, when not to sell at all.

If this book has done its job, it has not given you rules to follow blindly. It has given you a framework to think with, one that respects horses as living beings, buyers as human, and sellers as people who must live with the consequences of their decisions.

Selling horses the right way is not about avoiding risk altogether. It is about carrying it consciously and courteously.

Clear expectations, stated early and calmly, prevent resentment later. Most difficulties arise not because people disagree, but because they assumed.

The seller who communicates clearly, responds promptly, and holds boundaries consistently creates a process that feels fair, even when outcomes disappoint. That is what holds sales together.

That is what protects horses.

And that is what allows you to stand behind the decisions you make, long after the float has left the driveway.

One never forgets one's first sale.

This was of a lovely filly, my first foal. I bred her with the intention of keeping her, but she had pigeon toes and at the time of the sale was only 14.2h which was too small for me. My ideal height was 15.2h, the height of her mother. Her temperament was faultless and I had invested much time, care and training into her. I had no reference point as to how much a horse might grow after its two year old year.

So extremely reluctantly I put her on the market. She sold to the first enquirer and they took her away in the float that day. It was all so quick. I didn't have time to grieve. All I knew was that I had "betrayed" her by selling her, and all I had was the memories and a piece of paper (the cheque) in my hand.

I felt so empty.

I lived with the regret for some years. Fortunately I was able to buy her back when the owner's boys outgrew her, and she became an integral part of my broodmare band. She grew to 15.1h, and never produced a pigeon-toed foal.

The myth of the forever home

This piece addresses one of the most persistent ideas in horse selling: the promise of a forever home. While well intentioned, it is rarely realistic.

Horses outlive circumstances. People change. The ethical responsibility of the seller is not to guarantee the future, but to act responsibly at the point of transition.

What was learned

- There is no such thing as a guaranteed forever home
- Ethical selling is about process, not promises
- Good record keeping matters long after the sale
- Stepping back in when needed is part of responsibility

Related reading

“Selling horses – Can you really find a forever home?”

https://jeanettegower.substack.com/p/can-you-find-a-forever-home?utm_source=chatgpt.com

Afterword

When everything is done

Many times a sale leads to more than one can imagine.

Over the years, I have found that some buyers become colleagues, and sometimes friends. Not because that was intended, but because the placement was sound and communication stayed easy. Contact continues without any obligation. Excited updates are posted on Facebook. Buyers come back to see what else you might have.

I have watched horses go on to do far more than I could ever have offered them myself. Competing at levels and in disciplines I could not reach. Stepping into programs better suited to their strengths. Becoming part of breeding operations where their qualities are used thoughtfully and with care.

Some buyers check in from time to time. A message. A photograph. A short update on progress or training. These are never requirements. They are gestures, and they tend to arrive spontaneously.

I appreciate receiving photographs. When they are suitable for promotion or public use, I ask first. That preserves trust long after the sale.

Reputation tends to hold in the same way. Quietly. Without explanation. The people who need to know already do.

What I notice most, though, is what does *not* happen. I don't feel regret. I have no need to justify a decision. I don't have to wonder whether the horse will be fine. It has landed where it can progress without me. My role ends with peace of mind.

That, to me, is the mark of a sale well done.

You can contact the author at jeanette.gower@gmail.com or on Facebook at Chalani Australian Stock Horses, https://www.facebook.com/ChalaniStud/

Also by Jeanette Gower – Practical wisdom for all horse lovers

Buy The Right Horse

Buying a horse is exciting and full of promise, yet it is also a decision that shapes the years ahead. In *Buy The Right Horse*, Jeanette Gower offers a clear framework to help riders assess honestly and choose with confidence.

Drawing on decades of experience, she explains why suitability extends far beyond appearance or potential. Temperament, training, management, rider expectations, and future plans must align for a partnership to stay safe and satisfying.

Through structured questions, practical checklists, and real world examples, readers learn to recognise warning signs, communicate clearly with sellers, and interpret situations with confidence, grounding emotion in understanding.

A natural companion to *Sell Your Horse The Right Way*, this book helps buyers take responsibility for creating lasting matches that serve the rider, the seller, and most importantly, the horse.

The Rannock Legacy

In 2023, Rannock's induction into the Australian Stock Horse Society Hall of Fame marked the completion of a journey that began generations earlier. In *The Rannock Legacy*, Jeanette Gower records how one stallion's influence travelled across time, shaping horses, families, and breeding decisions far beyond his own years.

Drawing on careful research, photographs, and the recollections of those who knew his descendants, the book preserves a living thread within the breed. It is a record of continuity, respect, and the quiet transmission of qualities that still stand in paddocks and pedigrees today.

The Thinking Horse Breeder

Breeding horses asks more than enthusiasm. It asks for judgement, patience, and decisions that take years to prove themselves.

In *The Thinking Horse Breeder*, Jeanette Gower distills more than five decades of practical experience into a guide that helps breeders understand why some programs endure while others falter. Covering selection of stock, planning matings, inheritance, conformation, temperament, and the raising of young horses, the book moves step by step through the realities that shape long term success. Complex ideas are made usable, always grounded in what happens in paddocks, not just on paper.

With over 150 colour photographs, readers return to this work again and again as their knowledge deepens. What first appears straightforward reveals further layers of meaning with experience, making it a trusted companion from beginner stages through to established breeding operations.

Also available in Spanish as *Cría Equina Inteligente*, and as an *audiobook* edition, this modern classic continues to guide breeders with the same careful guidance on breeding decisions, planning, and long term responsibility that has supported owners around the world.

Homemade Dog Food Recipes

Feeding a dog well is one of the simplest and most meaningful ways owners show care, yet it can be difficult to know where to begin. In *Homemade Dog Food Recipes*, Jeanette Gower offers practical, balanced guidance designed for real homes and everyday routines.

It is more than just a recipe book. With clear instructions and economical ingredients, it helps owners build confidence in preparing meals that are science based and support long term well-being across different life stages.

All books available on Amazon.

About The Author

Jeanette Gower is an Australian Stock Horse breeder, educator, and author with more than fifty years of practical experience breeding, raising, and placing horses into suitable homes. Breeding under the *Chalani* prefix in South Australia, she and her daughter Kim have produced horses that have won throughout Australia.

For nineteen years Jeanette taught adult Equine Studies, helping owners make sense of breeding, training, and management decisions in ways that hold up in the real world. Her approach is grounded, thoughtful, and shaped by real outcomes rather than theory.

Across Jeanette's writing she returns to the same aim, helping people make careful, ethical choices they can stand behind, always with the horses in mind.

Practical frameworks for breeders, buyers, and sellers

Jeanette writes weekly *Reflections on 50+ Years of Horse Breeding*, where she shares practical insights, answers reader questions, and explores the realities behind breeding, buying, and selling horses. http://jeanettegower.substack.com

Find books and resources

Readers who would like to explore Jeanette's other work can find direct links, updates, and additional material through the sites below.

Resources:
https://jeanettegower.gumroad.com/

Books: https://thinkinghorsebreeder.chalani.net
and https://books.by/jeanette-gower

www.ingramcontent.com/pod-product-compliance
Ingram Content Group UK Ltd.
Pitfield, Milton Keynes, MK11 3LW, UK
UKHW020141250726
13967UKWH00002B/794

9 781968 253820